BODY LANGUAGE

BY JULIUS FAST

MJF BOOKS

NEW YORK

Published by MJF Books
Fine Communications
Two Lincoln Square
60 West 66th Street
New York, NY 10023

This book is gratefully dedicated to all the passengers of the second car in the Independent Subway's F train, eastbound from Fifth Avenue at 5:22 P.M.

ACKNOWLEDGMENTS
The author would like to express his appreciation to the following for their help in preparing this book:
Dr. Arnold Buchheimer, *Psychologist and Professor of Education at the City University of New York*; Dr. Albert E. Scheflen, *Professor of Psychiatry at the Albert Einstein College of Medicine*; Michael Wolff, *Doctoral candidate in Social Psychology, City University of New York*; Jean Linden, *Research Associate, Interscience Information, Inc.*

Library of Congress Catalog Card Number 92-60771
ISBN 1-56731-004-4

This edition published by arrangement with M. Evans & Co., Inc.

Manufactured in the United States of America

MJF Books and the MJF colophon are trademarks of Fine Creative Media, Inc.

10   9   8

Contents

1
The Body
is the Message

A Science Called Kinesics

Within the last few years a new and exciting science has been uncovered and explored. It is called body language. Both its written form and the scientific study of it have been labeled kinesics. Body language and kinesics are based on the behavioral patterns of nonverbal communication, but kinesics is still so new as a science that its authorities can be counted on the fingers of one hand.

Clinical studies have revealed the extent to which body language can actually contradict verbal communications. A classic example is the young woman who told her psychiatrist that she loved her boyfriend very much while nodding her head from side to side in subconscious denial.

Body language has also shed new light on the dynamics of interfamily relationships. A family sitting together, for example, can give a revealing picture of itself simply by the way its members move their arms and legs. If the mother crosses her legs first and the rest of the family then follows suit, she has set the lead for the family action, though she, as well as the rest of the family, may not be aware she is doing it. In fact her words may deny her leadership as she asks her husband or children for advice. But the unspoken, follow-the-leader clue in her action gives the family setup away to someone knowledgeable in kinesics.

A New Signal from The Unconscious

Dr. Edward H. Hess told a recent convention of the American College of Medical Hypnotists of a newly discovered kinesic signal. This is the unconscious widening of the pupil when the eye sees something pleasant. On a useful plane, this can be of help in a poker game if the player is in the "know." When his opponent's pupils widen, he can be sure that his opponent is holding a good hand. The player may not even be conscious of his ability to read this sign, any more than the other person is conscious of telegraphing his own luck.

Dr. Hess has found that the pupil of a normal man's eye becomes twice as large when he sees a picture of a nude woman.

On a commercial level, Dr. Hess cites the use of this new kinesic principle to detect the effect of an advertising commercial on television. While the commercial is being shown to a select audience, the eyes of the audience are photographed. The film is then later carefully studied to detect just when there is any widening of the eye; in other words, when there is any unconscious, pleasant response to the commercial.

Body language can include any non-reflexive or reflexive

movement of a part, or all of the body, used by a person to communicate an emotional message to the outside world. To understand this unspoken body language, kinesics experts often have to take into consideration cultural differences and environmental differences. The average man, unschooled in cultural nuances of body language, often misinterprets what he sees.

How to Tell the Girls Apart

Allen was a small-town boy who had come to visit Ted in the big city. One night, on his way to Ted's apartment and a big cocktail party, Allen saw a lovely young brunette walk across the street ahead of him and then start up the block. Allen followed her, marveling at the explicit quality of her walk. If ever Allen had seen a nonverbal message transmitted, this was it!

He followed her for a block, realizing that the girl was aware of him, and realizing too that her walk didn't change. Allen was sure this was a come-on.

Finally, at a red light, Allen summoned up his courage and catching up to the girl, gave her his pleasantest smile and said, "Hello."

To his amazement she turned a furious face to him and through clenched teeth said, "If you don't leave me alone I'll call a cop." Then as the light changed, she churned off.

Allen was stunned and scarlet with embarrassment. He hurried on to Ted's apartment where the party was in progress. While Ted poured him a drink he told him the story and Ted laughed. "Boy, you got the wrong number."

"But, hell, Ted—no girl at home would walk like that unless—unless she was asking for it."

"This is a Spanish-speaking neighborhood. Most of the

girls—despite outward appearances—are very good girls," Ted explained.

What Allen didn't understand is that in a culture, such as that of many Spanish-speaking countries, in which girls are chaperoned and there are strict codes of social behavior, a young girl can safely flaunt her sexuality without fear of inviting trouble. In fact, the walk that Allen took as a come-on would be considered only natural, and the erect, rigid posture of a proper American woman would probably be considered graceless and unnatural.

Allen circulated through the party and slowly forgot his humiliation.

As the party was breaking up, Ted cornered him and asked, "See anything you like?"

"That Janet," Allen sighed. "Man, I could really go for that—"

"Well, swell. Ask her to stay. Margie's staying too, and we'll have dinner."

"I don't know. She's just—like I couldn't get to first base with her."

"You're kidding."

"No. She's had the 'hands off' sign out all evening."

"But Janet likes you. She told me."

"But—" Bewildered, Allen said, "Then why is she so—so—I don't know, she just looks as if she didn't want me to lay a finger on her."

"That's Janet's way. You just didn't get the right message."

"I'll never understand this city," Allen said still bewildered, but happy.

As Allen found out, in Latin countries girls may telegraph a message of open sexual flirtation, and yet be so well chaperoned that any sort of physical "pass" is almost impossible. In countries where the chaperoning is looser, the girl will build her own defenses by a series of nonverbal messages that spell out "hands off." When the situation is such that a man cannot, within the rules of the culture, approach a strange girl on the street, a girl can move loosely and freely. In a city such as New York where a girl can expect almost anything, especially at a cocktail party, she learns to send out a message saying "hands off." To do this she will stand rigidly, cross her legs demurely when sitting, cross her arms over her breasts, and use other such defensive gestures.

The point is that for every situation there must be two elements to body language, the delivery of the message and the reception of the message. Had Allen been able to receive the messages correctly in terms of the big city he would have been spared the embarrassment of one encounter and could have avoided much of the uncertainty of the other.

To Touch or Not to Touch

Body language, in addition to sending and receiving messages, if understood and used adroitly can also serve to break through defenses. A businessman who was trying a bit too hard to wind up a very profitable deal found that he had misread the signs.

"It was a deal," he told me, "that would have been profitable not only to me but to Tom as well. Tom was in Salt Lake City from Bountiful, which isn't far away geographically, but is miles away culturally. It's a damned small town, and Tom was sure that everyone in the big city was out to take him. I think that deep down he was convinced that the deal was right for both of us, but he just couldn't trust my approach. I was the big city businessman, way up there, wheeling and dealing, and he was the small-time boy about to get rooked.

"I tried to cut through his image of the big city businessman by putting my arm around his shoulder. And that darn touch blew everything."

What my businessman friend had done was violate Tom's barrier of defenses with a nonverbal gesture for which the groundwork had not been laid. In body language he was trying to say, "Trust me. Let's make contact." But he only succeeded in committing a nonverbal assault. In ignoring Tom's defenses, the overeager businessman ruined the deal.

Often the swiftest and most obvious type of body language is touch. The touch of a hand, or an arm around someone's shoulder, can spell a more vivid and direct message than dozens of words. But such a touch must come at the right moment and in the right context.

Sooner or later every boy learns that touching a girl at the wrong moment may turn her off abruptly.

There are people who are "touchers," compulsive touchers, who seem completely impervious to all messages they may get from friends or companions. They are people who will touch and fondle others when they are bombarded with body language requests not to.

A Touch of Loneliness

However, touching or fondling in itself can be a potent signal. Touching an inanimate object can serve as a very loud and urgent signal, or a plea for understanding. Take the case of Aunt Grace. This old woman had become the center of a family discussion. Some of the family felt she would be better off in a pleasant and well-run nursing home nearby where she'd not only have people to take care of her but would also have plenty of companionship.

The rest of the family felt that this was tantamount to putting Aunt Grace "away." She had a generous income and a lovely apartment, and she could still do very well for herself. Why shouldn't she live where she was, enjoying her independence and her freedom?

Aunt Grace herself was no great help in the discussion. She sat in the middle of the family group, fondling her necklace and nodding, picking up a small alabaster paperweight and caressing it, running one hand along the velvet of the couch, then feeling the wooden carving.

"Whatever the family decides," she said gently. "I don't want to be a problem to anyone."

The family couldn't decide, and kept discussing the problem, while Aunt Grace kept fondling all the objects within reach.

Until finally the family got the message. It was a pretty obvious message too. It was just a wonder no one had gotten it sooner. Aunt Grace had been a fondler ever since she had begun living alone. She touched and caressed everything within reach. All the family knew it, but it wasn't until that moment that, one by one, they all became aware of what her fondling was saying. She was telling them in body language, "I am lonely. I am starved for companionship. Help me!"

Aunt Grace was taken to live with a niece and nephew, where she became a different woman.

Like Aunt Grace, we all, in one way or another, send our

little messages out to the world. We say, "Help me, I'm lonely. Take me, I'm available. Leave me alone, I'm depressed." And rarely do we send our messages consciously. We act out our state of being with nonverbal body language. We lift one eyebrow for disbelief. We rub our noses for puzzlement. We clasp our arms to isolate ourselves or to protect ourselves. We shrug our shoulders for indifference, wink one eye for intimacy, tap our fingers for impatience, slap our forehead for forgetfulness. The gestures are numerous, and while some are deliberate and others are almost deliberate, there are some, such as rubbing under our noses for puzzlement or clasping our arms to protect ourselves, that are mostly unconscious.

A study of body language is a study of the mixture of all body movements from the very deliberate to the completely unconscious, from those that apply only in one culture to those that cut across all cultural barriers.

2
Of Animals and Territory

The Symbolic Battle

The relationship between animal communication and human communication is only now beginning to be understood. Many of our insights into nonverbal communication have come from experiments with animals. Birds will communicate with each other by song, generation after generation singing the same set of notes, the same simple or complex melody. For many years scientists believed that these notes, these bird songs were hereditary accomplishments like the language of the porpoise, the language dances of certain wasps, and the "talking" of frogs.

Now, however, there is some doubt that this is completely so. Experiments seem to indicate that bird songs are learned. Scientists have raised certain birds away from any others of their own kind, and these fledglings have never been able to reproduce the species' typical songs.

Indeed the scientists who raised such birds were able to teach them a fragment of a popular song to replace the species song. Left alone, a bird like this would never be able to mate, for bird songs are involved with the entire mating process.

Another type of animal behavior that has long been termed instinctive is the symbolic fighting of dogs. When two male dogs meet they may react in a number of ways, but the most common is the snarling, snapping simulation of a fight to the death. The uninitiated onlooker will usually be alarmed by this behavior and may even try to separate the seemingly angry animals. The knowing dog owner simply watches, realizing how much of the fight is symbolic.

This is not to say that the fight isn't real. It is. The two animals are competing for mastery. One will win, because he is more aggressive, perhaps stronger and with harder drives than the other. The fight is over at the point when both dogs realize that one is the victor, though no skin has been broken. Then a curious thing happens. The vanquished dog lies down, rolls over and exposes his throat to the victor.

To this surrender, the victor reacts by simply standing over the vanquished, baring his fangs and growling for a definite period of time. Then both leap away and the battle is forgotten.

A nonverbal procedure has been acted out. The vanquished says, "I concede. You are the stronger and I bare my vulnerable throat to you."

The victor says, "Indeed, I am stronger and I will snarl and show that strength, but now let's get up and romp."

It is a curious aside to note that in almost no species of higher animal does one member of the species kill another for any reason, though they might fight with each other for many reasons. Among roe bucks at mating time such semi-symbolic fights can build up to the point of actual battle, and then, curiously, the animals will attack the nearby trees instead of each other.

Certain birds, after scolding and flapping in angry prelude to battle, will settle their differences by turning furiously to nest building. Antelope may lock horns and struggle for superiority, but the fight, however furious it may be, will end not always in death but in a ritual defeat. Animals have learned the art of acting out relationships in a kind of charade that is a first cousin to body language.

The controversial point about this symbolic battling behavior of dogs and other animals is whether this conduct, this type of communication, is inherited as instincts are inherited, imprinted in the genetic pattern of the species and handed down from generation to generation, or whether it is learned anew by each animal.

I mentioned that in some song birds the species' song must be learned; however, in others the songs are truly instinctive. Linnets learn their songs, while reed buntings inherit the ability to sing the characteristic species song whether or not they are in contact with other reed buntings during their growth. We must be careful in studying any behavior in the animal world not to generalize. What is true for one species of bird is not at all true for another. What is true for animals is not necessarily true for men. The symbolic battling of dogs is believed by many scientists to be an inherited thing, and yet I have had a dog trainer assure me that this behavior is learned.

"Watch a mother dog when her cubs are scrapping. If one is triumphant and tries to carry his victory to the point of damaging the other, the mother will immediately cuff him into neutrality, teaching him to respect the defeat of his brother. No, a dog must be taught symbolic behavior."

On the other hand there are dogs, such as the Eskimo dogs of Greenland, that seem to have a tremendous amount of difficulty learning symbolic behavior. Niko Tinbergen, the Dutch naturalist, says these dogs possess definite territories for each pack. Young male pups constantly violate the boundaries of these territories, and as a result they are constantly punished by the older males who have set the boundaries. The pups, however, never seem to learn just where the boundaries are. That is, until they reach sexual maturity.

From the time they experience their first copulation they suddenly become aware of the exact boundaries. Is this a learning process that has been reinforced over the years and now takes hold? Or is it some instinctive process that only develops with sexual maturity?

Can We Inherit Language?

The inheritance of instinct is not a simple matter, nor is the process of learning simple. It is difficult to pinpoint just how much of any system of communication is inherited and how much is learned. Not all behavior is learned, anymore than it is all inherited, even in humans.

And this brings us back to nonverbal communication. Are there universal gestures and expressions which are culturally independent and true for every human in every culture? Are there things every human being does which somehow communicate a meaning to all other humans regardless of race, color, creed or culture?

In other words, is a smile always indicative of amusement? Is a frown always a sign of displeasure? When we shake our head from side to side, does it always mean no? When we move it up and down, does it always mean yes? Are all these movements universal for all people, and if so, is the ability to make these movements in response to a given emotion inherited?

If we could find a complete set of inherited gestures and signals, then our nonverbal communication might be like the language of the porpoises or like the nonverbal language of the honeybee, who by certain definite motions can lead the entire hive population to a new-found supply of honey. These are inherited movements that the bee does not have to learn.

Have we an inherited form of communication?

Darwin believed that facial expressions of emotion are similar among humans, regardless of culture. He based his belief on man's evolutionary origin. Yet in the early 1950's, two researchers, Bruner and Taguiri, wrote, after thirty years of study, that the best available research indicated that there was no innate, invariable pattern accompanying specific emotions.

And then fourteen years later, three researchers, Ekman, Friesen (from California's Langley Porter Neuropsychiatric Institute) and Sorenson (from the National Institute of Neurological Diseases and Blindness) found that new research supported Darwin's old belief.

They had conducted studies in New Guinea, Borneo, the United States, Brazil and Japan, five widely different cultures on three different continents and discovered: "Observers in these cultures recognize some of the same emotions when they are shown a standard set of facial photographs."

According to the three men, this contradicts a theory that facial displays of emotion are socially learned. They also feel that there is agreement within a culture on recognizing different emotional states.

The reason they give for this universality of recognition is only indirectly related to inheritance. They cite a theory which postulates ". . . innate subcortical programs linking certain evokers to distinguishable universal facial displays for each of the primary affects—interest, joy, surprise, fear, anger, distress, disgust, contempt and shame."

In simpler words this means that the brains of all men are programmed to turn up the corners of the mouth when they're happy, turn them down when they're discontent, wrinkle the forehead, lift the eyebrows, raise one side of the mouth, and so forth and so on, according to what feeling is fed into the brain.

In opposition to this, they list other "culturally variable expressions and rules learned early in life."

"These rules," they say, "prescribe what to do about the display of each affect in different social settings; they vary with the social role and demographic characteristics and should vary across cultures."

The study that the three conducted tried as much as possible to avoid the conditioning that culture inflicts. The spread of television, movies and written matter makes this very difficult, but the investigators avoided much of this by studying isolated regions and, where they could, preliterate societies.

What their work proved seems to be the fact that we can inherit in our genetic makeup certain basic physical reactions. We are born with the elements of a nonverbal communication. We can make hate, fear, amusement, sadness and other basic feelings known to other human beings without ever learning how to do it.

Of course this does not contradict the fact that we must also learn many gestures that mean one thing in one society and something else in another society. We in the Western world shake our head from side to side to indicate no, and up and down to indicate yes, but there are societies in India where just the opposite is true. Up and down means no, and side to side means yes.

We can understand then that our nonverbal language is partly instinctive, partly taught and partly imitative. Later on we will see how important this imitative element is in nonverbal and verbal communication.

"The Territorial Imperative"

One of the things that is inherited genetically is the sense of territory. Robert Ardrey has written a fascinating book, *The Territorial Imperative,* in which he traces this territorial sense through the animal kingdom and into the human. In his book he discusses the staking out and guarding of territories by animals, birds, deer, fish and primates. For some species the territories are temporary, shifting with each season. For other animal species they are permanent. Ardrey makes an interesting case for the fact that, in his belief, "the territorial nature of man is genetic and ineradicable."

From his extensive animal studies he describes an innate code of behavior in the animal world that ties sexual reproduction to territorial defense. The key to the code, he believes, is territory, and the territorial imperative is the drive in animals and in men to take, hold and defend a given area.

There may be a drive in all men to have and defend a territory, and it may well be that a good part of that drive is inborn. However, we cannot always interpolate from humans to animals and from animals to humans.

The territorial imperative may exist in all animals and in some men. It may be strengthened by culture in some of these men and weakened in still others.

But there is little doubt that there is some territorial need in humans. How imperative it is remains to be seen. One of the most frightening plays of modern times is *Home*, by Megan Terry. It postulates a world of the future where the population explosion has caused all notion of territory to be discarded. All men live in cells in a gigantic metal hive enclosing the entire planet. They live out their lives, whole families confined to one room, without ever seeing sky or earth or another cell.

In this prophetic horror story, territory has been completely abolished. Perhaps this gives the play its great impact. In our modern cities we seem to be moving toward the abolition of territory. We find families crammed and boxed into rooms that are stacked one on another to dizzying heights. We ride elevators pressed together, and subway trains, packed in too tightly to move our arms or legs. We have yet to fully understand what happens to man when he is deprived of all territorial rights.

We know man has a sense of territory, a need for a shell of territory around him. This varies from the tight close shell of the city dweller through the larger bubble of yard and home in the suburbanite to the wide open spaces the country man enjoys.

How Much Space Does a Man Need?

We don't know how much space is necessary to any individual man, but what is important in our study of body language is what happens to any individual man when this shell of space or territory is threatened or breached. How does he respond and how does he defend it, or how does he yield?

I had lunch not too long ago with a psychiatrist friend. We sat in a pleasant restaurant at a stylishly small table. At one point he took out a pack of cigarettes, lit one and put the pack down three-quarters of the way across the table in front of my plate.

He kept talking and I kept listening, but I was troubled in some way that I couldn't quite define, and more troubled as he moved his tableware about, lining it up with his cigarettes, closer and closer to my side of the table. Then leaning across the table himself he attempted to make a point. It was a point I could hardly appreciate because of my growing uneasiness.

Finally he took pity on me and said, "I just favored you with a demonstration of a very basic step in body language, in nonverbal communication."

Puzzled, I asked, "What was that?"

"I aggressively threatened you and challenged you. I put you in a position of having to assert yourself, and that bothered you."

Still uncomprehending, I asked, "But how? What did you do?"

"I moved my cigarettes to start with," he explained. "By

unspoken rule we had divided the table in half, half for you and half for me."

"I wasn't conscious of any such division."

"Of course not. The rule remains though. We both staked out a territory in our minds. Ordinarily we would have shared the table by some unspoken and civilized command. However, I deliberately moved my cigarettes into your area in a breach of taste. Unaware of what I had done, you still felt yourself threatened, felt uneasy, and when I aggressively followed up my first breach of your territory with another, moving my plate and silverware and then intruding myself, you became more and more uneasy and still were not aware of why."

It was my first demonstration of the fact that we each possess zones of territory. We carry these zones with us and we react in different ways to the breaking of these zones. Since then I have tried out the same technique of cutting into someone else's zone when he was unaware of what I was doing.

At supper the other evening, my wife and I shared a table in an Italian restaurant with another couple. Experimentally I moved the wine bottle into my friend's "zone." Then slowly, still talking, followed up my intrusion by rearranging wine glass and napkin in his zone. Uneasily he shifted in his chair, moved aside, rearranged his plate, his napkin and finally in a sudden, almost compulsive lunge, moved the wine bottle back.

He had reacted by defending his zone and retaliating.

From this parlor game a number of basic facts emerge. No matter how crowded the area in which we humans live, each of us maintains a zone or territory around us—an inviolate area we try to keep for our own. How we defend this area and how we react to invasion of it, as well as how we encroach into other territories, can all be observed and charted and in many cases used constructively. These are all elements of nonverbal communication. This guarding of zones is one of the first basic principles.

How we guard our zones and how we aggress to other zones is an integral part of how we relate to other people.

3
How We Handle Space

A Space to Call Your Own

Among Quakers, the story is told of an urban Friend who visited a Meeting House in a small country town. Though fallen into disuse, it was architecturally a lovely building, and the city Quaker decided to visit it for Sunday meeting although he was told that only one or two Quakers still attended meetings there.

That Sunday he entered the building to find the meeting hall completely empty, the morning sun shafting through the old, twelve-paned windows, the rows of benches silent and unoccupied.

He slipped into a seat and sat there, letting the peaceful silence fill him. Suddenly he heard a slight cough and, looking up, saw a bearded Quaker standing near his bench, an old man who might well have stepped out of the pages of history.

He smiled, but the old Quaker frowned and coughed again,

then said, "Forgive me if I offend, but thee art sitting in my place."

The old man's quaint insistence on his own space, in spite of the empty meeting house, is amusing, but very true to life. Invariably, after you attend any church for any period of time, you stake out your own spot.

In his home Dad has his own particular chair, and while he may tolerate a visitor sitting there, it is often with poor grace. Mom has her own kitchen, and she doesn't like it one bit when her mother comes to visit and takes over "her" kitchen.

Men have their favorite seats in the train, their favorite benches in the park, their favorite chairs at conferences, and so on. It is all a need for territory, for a place to call one's own. Perhaps it is an inborn and universal need, though it is shaped by society and culture into a variety of forms. An office may be adequate for a working man or it may be too small, not according to the actual size of the room but according to placement of desk and chair. If the worker can lean back without touching a wall or a bookcase, it will usually seem big enough. But in a larger room, if his desk is placed so that he touches a wall when he leans back, the office may seem to be cramped from his viewpoint.

A Science Called Proxemics

Dr. Edward T. Hall, professor of anthropology at Northwestern University, has long been fascinated by man's reaction to the space about him, by how he utilizes that space and how his spatial use communicates certain facts and signals to other men. As Dr. Hall studied man's personal space, he coined the word *proxemics* to describe his theories and observations about zones of territory and how we use them.

Man's use of space, Dr. Hall believes, has a bearing on his ability to relate to other people, to sense them as being close or far away. Every man, he says, has his own territorial needs. Dr. Hall has broken these needs down in an attempt to standardize the science of proxemics and he has come up with four distinct zones in which most men operate. He lists these zones as 1) intimate distance, 2) personal distance, 3) social distance and 4) public distance.

As we might guess, the zones simply represent different areas we move in, areas that increase as intimacy decreases. Intimate distance can either be *close*, that is, actual contact, or *far*, from six to eighteen inches. The close phase of intimate distance is used for making love, for very close friendships and for children clinging to a parent or to each other.

When you are at *close intimate* distance you are overwhelmingly aware of your partner. For this reason, if such contact takes place between two men, it can lead to awkwardness or uneasiness. It is most natural between a man and a woman on intimate terms. When a man and a woman are not on intimate terms the close intimate situation can be embarrassing.

Between two women in our culture, a close intimate state is acceptable, while in an Arab culture such a state is acceptable between two men. Men will frequently walk hand in hand in Arab and in many Mediterranean lands.

The far phase of intimate distance is still close enough to clasp hands, but it is not considered an acceptable distance for two adult male Americans. When a subway or an elevator brings them into such crowded circumstances, they will automatically observe certain rigid rules of behavior, and by doing so communicate with their neighbors.

They will hold themselves as stiff as possible trying not to touch any part of their neighbors. If they do touch them, they either draw away or tense their muscles in the touching area. This action says, "I beg your pardon for intruding on your space, but the situation forces it and I will, of course, respect your privacy and let nothing intimate come of this."

If, on the other hand, they were to relax in such a situation and let their bodies move easily against their neighbors' bodies and actually enjoy the contact and the body heat, they would be committing the worst possible social blunder.

I have often seen a woman in a crowded subway car turn on an apparently innocent man and snarl, "Don't do that!" simply because the man had forgotten the rules and had relaxed against her. The snarls are worse when a man relaxes against another man.

Nor must we, in the crowded car or elevator, stare. There is a stated time interval during which we can look, and then we must quickly look away. The unwary male who goes beyond the stated time interval risks all sorts of unpleasant consequences.

I rode an elevator down in a large office building recently with another man. A pretty young girl got on at the fourteenth floor, and my friend looked at her absently but thoroughly. She grew redder and redder, and when the elevator stopped at the lobby, turned and snapped, "Haven't you ever seen a girl before, you—you dirty old man!"

My friend, still in his thirties, turned to me bewilderedly as she stormed out of the car and asked, "What did I do? Tell me, what the hell did I do?"

What he had done was to break a cardinal rule of nonverbal communication. "Look, and let your eyes slide away when you are in far intimate contact with a stranger."

The second zone of territory charted by Dr. Hall is called the *personal* distance zone. Here, too, he differentiates two areas, a *close personal* distance and a *far personal* distance. The close area is one and a half to two and a half feet. You can still hold or grasp your partner's hand at this distance.

As to its significance, he notes that a wife can stay within the close personal distance zone of her husband, but if another woman moves into this zone she presumably has designs on him. And yet this is obviously the comfortable distance at cocktail parties. It allows a certain intimacy and perhaps describes an intimate zone more than a personal zone. But since these are simply attempts by Dr. Hall to standardize a baby science, there may be a dozen clarifications before proxemics gets off the ground.

The far phase of personal distance, Dr. Hall puts at two and one half to four feet and calls this the limit of physical domination. You cannot comfortably touch your partner at this distance, and so it lends a certain privacy to any encounter. Yet the distance is close enough so that some degree of personal discussion can be held. When two people meet in the street, they usually stop at this distance from each other to chat. At a party they may tend to close in to the close phase of personal distance.

A variety of messages are transmitted by this distance and they range from, "I am keeping you at arm's length," to "I have singled you out to be a little closer than the other guests." To move too far in when you are on a *far personal* relationship with an acquaintance is considered pushy, or, depending on the sexual arrangement, a sign of personal favor. You make a statement with your distance, but the statement, to mean anything, must be followed up.

Social and Public Space

Social distance too has a close phase and a far phase. The *close* phase is four to seven feet and is generally the distance at which we transact impersonal business. It is the distance we assume when, in business, we meet the client from out of town, the new art director or the office manager. It is the distance the housewife keeps from the repairman, the shop clerk or the delivery boy. You assume this distance at a casual social gathering, but it can also be a manipulative distance.

A boss utilizes just this distance to dominate a seated employee—a secretary or a receptionist. To the employee, he tends to loom above and gain height and strength. He is, in fact, reinforcing the "you work for me" situation without ever having to say it.

The *far* phase of social distance, seven to twelve feet, is for more formal social or business relationships. The "big boss" will have a desk large enough to put him this distance from his employees. He can also remain seated at this distance and look up at an employee without a loss of status. The entire man is presented for his view.

To get back to the eyes, at this distance it is not proper to look briefly and look away. The only contact you have is visual, and so tradition dictates that you hold the person's eyes during conversation. Failing to hold his eyes is the same as excluding him from the conversation, according to Dr. Hall.

On the positive side, this distance allows a certain protection. You can keep working at this distance and not be rude, or you can stop working and talk. In offices it is necessary to preserve this far social distance between the receptionist and the visitor so that she may continue working without having to chat with him. A closer distance would make such an action rude.

The husband and wife at home in the evening assume this far social distance to relax. They can talk to each other if they wish or simply read instead of talking. The impersonal air of this type of social distance makes it an almost mandatory thing when a large family lives together, but often the family is arranged for this polite separation and must be pulled more closely together for a more intimate evening.

Finally, Dr. Hall cites *public* distance as the farthest extension of our territorial bondage. Again there is a close phase and a far phase, a distinction which may make us wonder why there aren't eight distances instead of four. But actually, the distances are arrived at according to human interaction, not to measurement.

The *close* phase of public distance is twelve to twenty-five feet, and this is suited for more informal gatherings, such as a teacher's address in a roomful of students, or a boss at a conference of workers. The *far* phase of public distance, twenty-five feet or more, is generally reserved for politicians where the distance is also a safety or a security factor, as it is with animals. Certain animal species will let you come only within this distance before moving away.

While on the subject of animal species and distance, there is always the danger of misinterpreting the true meaning of distance and territorial zones. A typical example is the lion and the lion tamer. A lion will retreat from a human when the human comes too close and enters his "danger" zone. But when he can retreat no longer and the human still advances, the lion will turn and approach the human.

A lion tamer takes advantage of this and moves toward

the lion in his cage. The animal retreats, as is its nature, to the back of the cage as the lion tamer advances. When the lion can go no farther, he turns and, again in accordance with his nature, advances on the trainer with a snarl. He invariably advances in a perfectly straight line. The trainer, taking advantage of this, puts the lion's platform between himself and the lion. The lion, approaching in a straight line, climbs on the platform to get at the trainer. At this point the trainer quickly moves back out of the lion's danger zone, and the lion stops advancing.

The audience watching this interprets the gun that the trainer holds, the whip and the chair in terms of its own inner needs and fantasies. It feels that he is holding a dangerous beast at bay. This is the nonverbal communication of the entire situation. This, in body language, is what the trainer is trying to tell us. But here body language lies.

In actuality, the dialogue between lion and tamer goes like this—Lion: "Get out of my sphere or I'll attack you." Trainer: "I am out of your sphere." Lion: "All right. I'll stop right here."

It doesn't matter where *here* is. The trainer has manipulated things so that *here* is the top of the lion's platform.

In the same way the far public sphere of the politician or the actor on a stage contains a number of body language statements which are used to impress the audience, not necessarily to tell the truth.

It is at this far public distance that it is difficult to speak the truth or, to turn it around, at this far public distance it is most easy to lie with the motions of the body. Actors are well aware of this, and for centuries they have utilized the distance of the stage from the audience to create a number of illusions.

At this distance the actor's gestures must be stylized, affected and far more symbolic than they are at closer public, social or intimate distances.

On the television screen, as in the motion picture, the combination of long shots and close-ups calls for still another type of body language. A movement of the eyelid or the eyebrow or a quiver of the lip in a close-up can convey as much of a message as the gross movement of arm or an entire body in a long shot.

In the close-up the gross movements are usually lost. This may be one of the reasons television and motion picture actors have so much trouble adapting to the stage.

The stage often calls for a rigid, mannered approach to acting because of the distance between actors and audience. Today, in revolt against this entire technique, there are elements of the theatre that try to do away with the public distance between actor and stage.

They either move down into the audience, or invite the audience up to share the stage with them. Drama, under these conditions, must be a lot less structured. You can have no assurance that the audience will respond in the way you wish. The play therefore becomes more formless, usually without a plot and with only a central idea.

Body language, under these circumstances, becomes a difficult vehicle for the actor. He must on the one hand drop many of the symbolic gestures he has used, because they just won't work over these short distances. He cannot rely on natural body language for the emotions he wishes to project no matter how much he "lives" his part. So he must develop a new set of symbols and stylized body motions that will also lie to the audience.

Whether this "close-up" lying will be any more effective than the far-off lying of the proscenium stage remains to be seen. The gestures of the proscenium or traditional stage have been refined by years of practice. There is also a cultural attachment involved with the gestures of the stage. The Japanese kabuki theater, for example, contains its own refined symbolic gestures that are so culture-oriented that more than half of them may be lost on a Western audience.

How Different Cultures Handle Space

There are, however, body languages that can transcend cultural lines. Charlie Chaplin's little tramp, in his silent movies, was universal enough in his movements to bring almost every culture to laughter, including the technologically unsophisticated cultures of Africa. However, culture is still a guiding factor in all body language, and this is particularly true of body zones. Dr. Hall goes into the cross-cultural implication of his proxemics. In Japan, for example, crowding together is a sign of warm and pleasant intimacy. In certain situations, Hall believes the Japanese prefer crowding.

Donald Keene, who wrote *Living Japan*, notes the fact that in the Japanese language there is no word for privacy. Still this does not mean that there is no concept of privacy. To the Japanese, privacy exists in terms of his house. He regards this area as his own and resents intrusion into it. The fact that he crowds together with other people does not negate his need for living space.

Dr. Hall sees this as a reflection of the Japanese concept of space. Westerners, he believes, see space as the distance between objects. To us, space is empty. The Japanese see the shape and arrangement of space as having a tangible meaning. This is apparent not only in their flower arrangements and art, but in their gardens as well, where units of space blend harmoniously to form an integrated whole.

Like the Japanese, the Arabs too tend to cling close to one another. But while in public they are invariably crowded together, in private, in their own houses, the Arabs have almost too much space. Arab houses are, if possible, large and empty, with the people clustered together in one small area. Partitions between rooms are usually avoided, because in spite of the desire for space, the Arabs, paradoxically, do not like to be alone and even in their spacious houses will huddle together.

The difference between the Arab huddling and the Japanese proximity is a deep thing. The Arab likes to touch his companion, to feel and to smell him. To deny a friend his breath is to be ashamed.

The Japanese, in their closeness, preserve a formality and an aloofness. They manage to touch and still keep rigid boundaries. The Arab pushes these boundaries aside.

Along with this closeness, there is a pushing and a sharing in the Arab world that Americans find distasteful. To an American there are boundaries in a public place. When he is waiting in line he believes that his place there is inviolate. The Arab has no concept of privacy in a public place, and if he can push his way into a line, he feels perfectly within his rights to do so.

As the Japanese lack of a word for privacy indicates a certain attitude toward other people, so the Arab lack of a word for rape indicates a certain attitude toward the body. To an American the body is sacred. To the Arab, who thinks nothing of shoving and pushing and even pinching women in public, violation of the body is a minor thing. However, violation of the ego by insult is a major problem.

Hall points out that the Arab at times needs to be alone, no matter how close he wishes to be to his fellow man. To be alone, he simply cuts off the lines of communication. He withdraws, and this withdrawal is respected by his fellows. His withdrawal is interpreted in body language as "I need privacy. Even though I'm among you, touching you and living with you, I must withdraw into my shell."

Were the American to experience this withdrawal, he would tend to think it insulting. The withdrawal would be interpreted in his body language as "silent treatment." And it would be further interpreted as an insult.

When two Arabs talk to each other, they look each other in the eyes with great intensity. The same intensity of glance in our American culture is rarely exhibited between men. In fact, such intensity can be interpreted as a challenge to a man's masculinity. "I didn't like the way he looked at me, as if he wanted something personal, to sort of be too intimate," is a typical response by an American to an Arab look.

The Western World's Way with Space

So far we have considered body language in terms of spatial differences in widely disparate cultures, the East and Near East as opposed to the West. However, even among the Western nations, there are broad differences. There is a distinct difference between the way a German, for instance, handles his living space, and the way an American does. The American carries his two-foot bubble of privacy around with him, and if a friend talks to him about intimate matters they will come close enough for their special bubbles to merge. To a German, an entire room in his own house can be a bubble of privacy. If someone else engages in an intimate conversation in that room without including him he may be insulted.

Perhaps, Hall speculates, this is because in contrast to the Arab, the German's ego is "extraordinarily exposed." He will therefore go to any length to preserve his private sphere. In World War II, German prisoners of war were housed four to a hut in one army camp. Hall notes that as soon as they could they set about partitioning their huts to gain private space. In open stockades, German prisoners tried to build their own private dwelling units.

The German's "exposed ego" may also be responsible for a stiffness of posture and a general lack of spontaneous body movement. Such stiffness can be a defense or mask against revealing too many truths by unguarded movements.

In Germany, homes are constructed for a maximum of privacy. Yards are well-fenced and balconies are screened. Doors are invariably kept closed. When an Arab wants privacy he retreats into himself but when a German wants privacy he retreats behind a closed door. This German desire for privacy, for a definite private zone that does not intrude on anyone else's, is typified by his behavior in line-ups or queues.

At a movie house in a German-American neighborhood I waited in line recently for a ticket and listened to the German conversation about me as we moved forward in neat and orderly fashion.

Suddenly, when I was just a few places from the ticket-seller's window, two young men who, I later learned, were Polish walked up to the head of the line and tried to buy their tickets immediately.

An argument broke out around us. "Hey! We've been waiting on line. Why don't you?"

"That's right. Get back in line."

"To hell with that! It's a free country. Nobody asked you to wait in line," one of the Poles called out, forcing his way to the ticket window.

"You're queued up like sheep," the other one said angrily. "That's what's wrong with you Krauts."

The near riot that ensued was brought under control by two patrolmen, but inside the lobby I approached the line crashers.

"What were you trying to do out there? Start a riot?"

One of them grinned. "Just shaking them up. Why form a line? It's easier when you mill around." Discovering that they were Polish helped me understand their attitude. Unlike the Germans, who want to know exactly where they stand and feel that only orderly obedience to certain rules of conduct guarantees civilized behavior, the Poles see civilized behavior as a flouting of authority and regulations.

While the Englishman is unlike the German in his treatment of space—he has little feeling for the privacy of his own room—he is also unlike the American. When the American wishes to withdraw he goes off by himself. Possibly because of the lack of private space and the "nursery" raising of children in England, the Englishman who wants to be alone tends to withdraw into himself like the Arab.

The English body language that says, "I am looking for some momentary privacy" is often interpreted by the American as, "I am angry at you, and I am giving you the silent treatment."

The English social system achieves its privacy by carefully structured relationships. In America you speak to your next door neighbor because of proximity. In England, being a neighbor to someone does not at all guarantee that you know them or speak to them.

There is the story of an American college graduate who met an English Lady on an ocean liner to Europe. The boy was seduced by the Englishwoman and they had a wild affair.

A month later he attended a large and very formal dinner in London and among the guests, to his delight, he saw Lady X. Approaching her he said, "Hello! How have you been?"

Looking down her patrician nose, Lady X drawled, "I don't think we've been introduced."

"But . . . ," the bewildered young man stammered, "surely you remember me?" Then emboldened, he added, "Why, only last month we slept together on the trip across."

"And what," Lady X asked icily, "makes you think that constitutes an introduction?"

In England relationships are made not according to physical closeness but according to social standing. You are not necessarily a friend of your neighbor unless your social backgrounds are equal. This is a cultural fact based on the heritage of the English people, but it is also a result of the crowded condition in England. The French, like the English, are also crowded together, but their different cultural heritage has produced a different cultural result. While crowding has caused the English to develop an inordinate respect for privacy, it has caused the French to be very much involved with each other.

A Frenchman meets your eyes when he is talking to you, and he looks at you directly. In Paris women are closely examined visually on the streets. In fact many American women returning from Paris feel suddenly unappreciated. The Frenchman, by his look, conveys a nonverbal message. "I like you. I may never know you or speak to you, but I appreciate you."

No American male looks at women like this. Instead of appreciation this would be interpreted as rudeness in an American.

In France the crowding is partly responsible for the Frenchmen's involvement with each other. It is also held responsible for their concern with space. French parks treat space differently than American parks do. They have a reverence for their open areas, a reverence even in the city, for the beauty of architecture.

We react to space in a different fashion. In New York we are an intensely crowded city and because of this we have developed an individual need for privacy. The New Yorker is traditionally known for his "unfriendly attitude" and yet the unfriendly attitude is developed out of a respect for our neighbor's privacy. We will not intrude on that privacy, so we ignore each other in elevators, in subways, on crowded streets.

We march along in our own little worlds, and when those worlds are forced together we go into a catatonic state to avoid a misinterpretation of our motives.

In body language we scream, "I am being forced to rub up against you, but my rigidity tells you that I do not mean to intrude." Intrusion is the worst sin. Speak to a stranger in New York City and you get a startled, alarmed reaction.

Only in times of great crisis do the barriers fall down, and then we realize that New Yorkers are not unfriendly at all, but rather shy and frightened. During the Great Northeast Power Failure everybody reached out to everybody else, to help, to comfort, to encourage and for a few warm, long hours the city was a vital place.

Then the lights went on and we fell back into our rigid zones of privacy.

Out of New York, in small American towns, there is a more

open friendly attitude. People will say, "Hello," to strangers, smile and often make conversation. However, in *very* small towns, where everyone knows everyone else and there is very little privacy, the stranger may be treated to the same stand-offish attitude that he receives in the very big city.

4
When Space
is Invaded

Defending Body Zones

At first glance it might be hard to see the exact relationship between personal spaces, zones or territories and kinesics, body language. But unless we understand the basic principles of individual territories we cannot appreciate what happens when these territories are invaded. How we react to personal invasion of our territory is very much related to body language. We should know our own aggressive behavior and our reactions to others' aggressions if we are to become aware of what signals we are sending and receiving.

Perhaps the most touching account of the inviolability of body zones was a novel written almost half a century ago by H. DeVere Stacpool, called *The Blue Lagoon*. It is the story of a young child shipwrecked on a tropical island with an old sailor. The sailor raises the boy to self-sufficiency and then dies, and the child grows to manhood alone, meets a young Polynesian girl and falls in love with her. The novel deals with the boy's love affair with the Polynesian girl who has been declared taboo from infancy. She has grown up forbidden to allow herself to be touched by any man. The struggle between the two to break down her conditioning and allow him to touch her makes a fascinating and moving story.

It was the early recognition of just how defensive a human can become about his body zones and personal privacy that led Stacpool to explore this theme, but it has only been in the last decade that scientists have begun to understand the complex significance of personal space.

In an earlier chapter I told of a psychiatrist who, with the aid of a pack of cigarettes, taught me a lesson about the invasion of personal space. He in turn had learned much of what he knew from the reaction of patients in hospitals for the mentally ill. A mental hospital is a closed microcosm, and as such often reflects and exaggerates attitudes of the larger world outside. But a mental hospital is also a very special type of place. The inmates are more susceptible to suggestion and aggression than are normal men and women and often their actions distort the actions of normal people.

How aggressive a mental patient is to someone depends on the rank of the other person. It is a test of dominance. In any mental hospital one or two patients will attain superior rank by aggressive behavior, but they can always be cowed by one of the attendants. In turn, the attendant is beneath the nurse and she is subordinate to the doctor.

There is a very real hierarchy developed in these institutions and it is reflected in the outer world in organizations like the army, or in business where there is a definite order of dominance. In the army, dominance is achieved by a system of symbols, stripes for the noncommissioned officers and bars, leaves, birds and stars for the commissioned officers. But even without the symbols, the pecking order remains. I have seen privates in a shower room deferential to sergeants without knowing who they were or what their rank was. The sergeants, through their manner and bearing, were able to convey an obvious body language message of rank.

Advice For Status Seekers

In the business world, where neither stripes nor other obvious symbols are worn, the same ability to project a sense of superiority is the common attainment of the executive. How does he do it? What tricks does he use to subdue subordinates, and what tricks does he bring out for in-fighting in his own rank?

An attempt to study this was made by two researchers in a series of silent films. They had two actors play the parts of an executive and a visitor, and switch roles for different takes. The scene had one man at his desk while the other, playing the part of a visitor, knocks at the door, opens it and approaches the desk to discuss some business matter.

The audience watching the films was asked to rate the executive and the visitor in terms of status. A certain set of rules began to emerge from the ratings. The visitor showed the least amount of status when he stopped just inside the door to talk across the room to the seated man. He was considered to have more status when he walked halfway up to the desk, and he had most status when he walked directly up to the desk and stood right in front of the seated executive.

Another factor that governed status in the eyes of the observers was the time between knocking and entering, and for the seated executive, the time between hearing the knock and answering. The quicker the visitor entered the room, the more status he had. The longer the executive took to answer, the more status *he* had.

It should be obvious that what is involved here is a matter of territory. The visitor is allowed to enter the executive's territory, and by that arrangement the executive automatically achieves superior status.

How far into the territory the visitor penetrates, and how quickly he does it, in other words how he challenges the personal space of the executive, announces his own status.

The "big boss" will walk into his subordinate's office unannounced. The subordinate will wait outside the boss's office until he is permitted in. If the boss is on the phone, the subordinate may tiptoe off and come back later. If the subordinate is on the phone, the boss will usually assert his status by standing above the subordinate until he murmurs, "Let me call you back," and then gives the boss his full attention.

There is a continuous shifting or fighting for status within the business world, and therefore status symbols become a very necessary part of the shift or dance. The executive with the attaché case is the most obvious one, and we all know the joke of the man who carries only his lunch in his attaché case but insists on carrying the case simply because it is so important to the image he must project. I know of a black minister and educator in America who travels around the country a great deal. He told me that he would never go into any Southern city, into the downtown area or a hotel, without a business suit and an attaché case. These two symbols gave him a certain amount of authority that differentiated him from the "nigger" in the same city.

Big business sets up a host of built-in status symbols. A large drug firm in Philadelphia earned enough money through the sale of tranquilizers to put up a new building that would house their rapidly expanding staff. The building could have been designed with any number of offices and workrooms, but quite deliberately the company set up a built-in status symbol in the offices. The corner offices on the very highest floor were reserved for the very highest personnel. The corner offices on the floor below were reserved for the next rank of top personnel. Lesser, but still important executives had offices without corner windows. The rank below this had offices without windows at all. Below them were the men with partitioned cubicles for offices. These had frosted glass walls and no doors and the next rank down had clear glass cubicles. The last rank had desks out in an open room.

Rank was arrived at by an equation whose elements consisted of time on the job, importance of the job, salary and degree. The degree of M.D., for example, gave any man, no matter what his salary or time on the job, the right to have a closed office. Ph.D.'s might or might not have such an office, depending on other factors.

Within this system there was room for many other elements to demonstrate degree of status. Drapes, rugs, wooden desks as opposed to metal desks, furniture, couches, easy chairs, and of course, secretaries, all set up subhierarchies.

An important element in this set-up was the contrast between the frosted glass cubicles and the clear glass cubicles. By allowing the world to see in, the man in the clear glass cubicle was automatically reduced in importance or rank. His territory was that much more open to visual invasion. He was that much more vulnerable.

How to Be a Leader

Opening of territory and invasion of territory are important functions of rank in business. What about leadership? By what tricks or by what body language does a leader assert himself?

Back in the years just before World War II, Charlie Chaplin did a motion picture called *The Great Dictator*. As with all of Chaplin's movies, it was filled with bits of body language, but the most delightful sequence was one that took place in a barber shop.

Chaplin as Hitler and Jack Oakie as Mussolini are shown getting shaves in adjacent chairs. The scene centers around the attempts of each to put himself in a dominant position to the other in order to assert his superior leadership. Trapped within their chairs, lathered and draped, there is only one way to achieve dominance, and that is by controlling the height of the chairs. They can reach down and jack them up. The higher man wins, and the scene revolves around the attempt of each to jack his own chair to a higher position.

Dominance through height is a truism that works from the animal kingdom to man. Among wolves, recent studies have shown that the pack leader asserts his dominance by wrestling a yearling or subordinate wolf to the ground and standing over him. The subordinate expresses his subservience by crawling beneath the pack leader and exposing his throat and belly. It becomes a matter of who is higher.

The same positioning occurs with humans. We are all aware of the tradition of abasement before a king, before idols, before altars. Bowing and scraping in general are all variations of superiority or inferiority by height. They are all actions to point out the body language message, "You are higher than I am, therefore you are dominant."

A young man I know, well over six feet tall, was extremely successful in business because of his ability to show empathy for his associates. Observing him in action in some successful business transactions I became aware that whenever possible he stooped, sloped his body, or sat, in order to allow his associate to achieve dominance and feel superior.

In family seatings the dominant member, usually the father, will hold sway at the head of a rectangle table or an oval table. Often the choice of a round table will tell something of the family set-up. In the same way in discussion groups around a table, the leader will automatically assume the head of the table position.

That this is no new concept is obvious in the story of King Arthur and his round table. The table was round so that there could be no question of dominance and every knight could share equally in the honor of being seated at the table. However, this whole idea was weakened by the fact that Arthur himself, wherever he sat, became the dominant figure and status decreased as the distance from the King increased.

The boss of a large drug company I have worked in has an office that contains, in addition to his desk and desk chair, a couch, an easy chair and a coffee table with one or two chairs around it. This man announces the formality or informality of a situation by where he sits during that situation. If a visitor comes whom he wants to treat in an informal manner, he will come around from his desk and guide the visitor to the couch, to the easy chair or to the coffee table. In this way, by his positioning, he indicates just what type of interview he will have. If it's to be an extremely formal one he will remain seated behind his desk.

The Space We Hold Inviolate

The need for personal space and the resistance to the invasion of personal space is so strong a thing that even in a crowd each member will demand a given amount of space. This very fact led a journalist named Herbert Jacobs to attempt to apply it to crowd size. Since estimation of crowd size tends to vary according to whether the observer is for the crowd or against it, the size of political rallies, peace rallies and demonstrations are inflated by the marchers and deflated by the authorities.

Jacobs, by studying aerial photographs of crowds where he could actually count heads, concluded that people in dense crowds need six to eight square feet each, while people in loose crowds require an average of ten square feet. Crowd size, Jacobs finally concluded, could be gauged by the formula, *length* times *width* divided by a *correction factor* that took density of the crowd into account. This gave the actual number of people in any gathering.

On the subject of crowds, it is important to realize that the personal territory of the people in a crowd is destroyed by the very act of crowding. The reaction to this destruction can, in some cases, change the temper of the crowd. Men react very strongly when their personal space or territory is invaded. As a crowd gets larger and tighter and more compact, it may also get uglier. A loose crowd may be easier to handle.

This need for personal space was known to Freud, who always arranged his sessions so that the patient would lie on the couch while he sat in a chair out of the patient's sight.

In this way there was no intrusion upon the patient's personal space.

The police are also well aware of this fact, and they take advantage of it in their interrogation of prisoners. A textbook on criminal interrogation and confessions suggests that the questioner sit close to the suspect and that there be no table or other obstacle between them. Any kind of obstacle, the book warns, gives the man being questioned a certain degree of relief and confidence.

The book also suggests that the questioner, though he may start with his chair two or three feet away, should move in closer as the questioning proceeds, so that "ultimately one of the subject's knees is just about in between the interrogator's two knees."

This physical invasion of the man's territory by the police officer, the crowding in as he is questioned, has been found in practice to be extremely useful in breaking down a prisoner's resistance. When a man's territorial defenses are weakened or intruded upon, his self-assurance tends to grow weaker.

In a working situation the boss who is aware of this can strengthen his own position of leadership by intruding spatially on the man under him. The higher-up who leans over the subordinate's desk throws the subordinate off balance. The department head who crowds next to the worker while inspecting his work makes the worker uneasy and insecure. In fact, the parent who scolds the child by leaning over him is compounding the relationship between them, proving and reinforcing his own dominance.

Can we use this intrusion of personal space to arouse defensive measures in others, or can we, by avoiding it, also avoid the sometimes dangerous consequences of an intrusion? We know that tailgating a car is dangerous from a purely physical point of view. If the car ahead stops short we can smack into it, but no one talks about what the act of tailgating can do to the nerves of the driver ahead.

A man driving a car often loses an essential part of his own humanity and is, by virtue of the machine around him, once removed from a human being. The body language communication that works so well for him outside the car often will not work at all when he is driving. We have all been annoyed by drivers who cut in front of us, and we all know the completely irrational rage that can sometimes fill the driver who has thus had his space invaded. The police will cite statistics to show that dozens of accidents are caused by this cutting in, by the dangerous reaction of the man who has been cut off. In a social situation few men would dream of acting or reacting in this fashion. Stripped of the machine we adopt a civilized attitude and allow people to cut in front of us, indeed we step aside quite often to permit people to board a bus or elevator ahead of us.

A car, however, seems to act much like a dangerous weapon in the hands of many drivers. It can become a weapon that destroys many of our controls and inhibitions. The reason for this is obscure, but some psychologists have theorized that at least a part of it is due to the extension of our personal territories when we are in a car. Our own zones of privacy expand and the zone of privacy of the car becomes much greater and our reaction to any intrusion on that zone is greater still.

Of Space and Personality

There have been many studies attempted to find out just how the reaction to invasion of personal space is related to personality. One, a master's thesis by John L. Williams, determined that introverts tended to keep people at a greater conversational distance than extroverts. The man who is withdrawn needs greater defenses to insure the sanctity of his withdrawn state. Another study, for a doctoral thesis, by William E. Leipold arrived at the same conclusion by a clever experiment. Students were first given personality tests to see if they were introverted or extroverted, and then were sent to an office to be interviewed about their grades.

Three types of instructions to the students were given by the experimenter. These were called *stress, praise* or *neutral* instructions. The stress instructions were geared to upset the man. "We feel that your course grade is quite poor and that you haven't tried your best. Please take a seat in the next room till the interviewer can speak to you."

The student then entered a room with a desk and two chairs, one in front of it and one behind it.

The praise interview started with the student being told that his grades were good and that he was doing well. In the neutral interview the instructions were simply, "We are interested in your feelings about the course."

Results of the study showed that the students who were praised sat closest to the interviewer's chair. The students under stress sat farthest away, and the ones receiving neutral instructions sat midway. Introverted and anxious students sat farther away than extroverted students under the same conditions.

With this much charted, the next step was to determine the reactions of men and women when their territory was invaded. Dr. Robert Sommer, professor of psychology and chairman of the Psychology Department at the University of California, describes a set of experiments conducted in a hospital environment where, dressed in a doctor's white coat to gain authority, he systematically invaded the patients' privacy, sitting next to them on benches and entering their wards and day rooms. These intrusions, he reported, invariably bothered the patients and drove them from their special chairs or areas. The patients reacted to Dr. Sommer's physical intrusion by becoming uneasy and restless and finally by removing themselves bodily from the area.

From his own observations and the observations of others Dr. Sommer has discovered a whole area of body language that the individual uses when his private territory is invaded. Aside from the actual physical retreat of picking up and going somewhere else, there will be a series of preliminary signals, rocking, leg swinging or tapping. These are the first signs of tension, and they say, "You are too near. Your presence makes me uneasy."

The next series of body language signals are closed eyes, withdrawal of the chin into the chest and hunching of the shoulders. These all say, "Go away. I do not want you here. You are intruding."

Dr. Sommer tells of another researcher into the field of spatial invasion, Nancy Russo, who used a library as her theater of operations. A library is a perfect place to observe reactions. It is a subdued atmosphere geared to privacy. In most cases a newcomer to a library will isolate himself from the other researchers by taking a seat some distance from anyone else.

Miss Russo would take an adjacent chair and then move closer to her victim, or sit across from him. While she found no single universal reaction to people sitting close, she found that most spoke with body language to transmit their feelings. She described "defensive gestures, shifts in posture, attempts to move away unobtrusively." Eventually, she concluded, if all of a man's body language signals are ignored, he will take off and move to another location.

Only one out of eighty students whose area was intruded on by Miss Russo asked her verbally to move away. The rest used body language to communicate their disapproval of the closeness.

Dr. Augustus F. Kinzel, who now works at the New York Psychiatric Institute, evolved a theory while working at the U.S. Medical Center for Federal Prisoners which may point the way toward detecting, predicting and even treating violent behavior in men.

In his early animal studies Dr. Kinzel noted that animals will often react with violence to any intrusion of their personal territory. While working at the prison in a population selected for violent action against society, he noticed that certain men preferred isolation cells despite the deprivations of such living. He found that these same men were sometimes troubled by senseless outbursts of violence. Could it be that these men required more space to maintain their self-control?

Dr. Kinzel found that many men who were guilty of assault with violence complained that their victims had "messed around with them," though a careful check disclosed that they had assaulted men who had done nothing but come close to them. The fits of violence were similarly provoked in and out of prison, so the prison atmosphere could not explain it. What could?

To find out, Dr. Kinzel conducted an experiment in the prison with fifteen volunteer prisoners. Eight had violent histories and seven didn't. The men were asked to stand in the center of an empty room while the "experimenter" approached them slowly. Each was to say, "Stop!" when the experimenter came too close.

When the experiment was repeated again and again, each man was found to have a definite body zone, territory or bubble, a personal space Dr. Kinzel labeled a "body buffer zone."

"The violent group," Dr. Kinzel said, "kept the experimenter at twice the distance the non-violent ones did." Their body buffer zones were four times larger in volume than the zones of the non-violent group. When someone got too close to one of these men, he resisted as though the intruder were "looming up" or "rushing in."

In this experiment the same feeling had been induced in the violent men as when they had assaulted other prisoners for "messing around." These men, Dr. Kinzel decided, went into an unreal panic when someone intruded upon their larger-than-normal body zones. This panic and its resulting violence occurred at a distance that other people would consider normal.

Much of what Dr. Kinzel calls "the quickly spiraling character of violence between 'overcrowded' ghetto groups and the police" may be due to a poor understanding by the police of the sanctity of body zones. Dr. Kinzel's study seems to indicate that we are only beginning to understand the origins of violent outbreaks in human beings, and how to detect and manage them, outbreaks which seldom occur in the animal kingdom where a tacit understanding of territorial needs exists until man interferes.

Sex and Non-Persons

There is, in the whole business of invasion, a strong sexual link. A girl moving into a man's territory encounters a different set of signals than if she were moving into a woman's territory. There is more acceptance and the possibility of a flirtation makes the man less likely to resent the intrusion. The same situation reversed, however, generally puts a woman on her guard.

The signal that invariably is sent by intruders is, "You are a non-person, and therefore I can move in on you. You do not matter."

This signal, in the context of a business situation between boss and employee, can be demoralizing to the employee and useful to the boss. It can in fact reaffirm the boss's leadership.

In a crowded subway there is a slightly different interpretation of the signals. There it is important that the two people regard each other as non-persons. Otherwise the fact that they are forced into such intimate terms may be awkward. The person who intrudes on another verbally in a crowded subway is guilty of a gaucherie. It may in fact be a little left of gauche. Here a rigid withdrawal is necessary in order to endure an uncomfortable situation. We have never seen any movies in which a boy and a girl meet on a crowded subway. It just isn't done, even in Hollywood.

The crowding in subway trains is only bearable, Sommer believes, because the riders tend to think of each other as non-persons. If they are forced to acknowledge each other's presence because of an abrupt stop, for instance, they may resent the situation in which they find themselves.

The reverse is also true. In an uncrowded situation a person will resent being treated as a non-person. Our library researcher noticed one man who lifted his head and stared at her coldly, signaling with body language, "I am an individual, by what right do you intrude?"

He was using body language to resist her intrusion and

she all at once became the person aggressed against, instead of the aggressor. So strongly did she feel this man's disapproval that she was unable to follow through her experiment for the rest of that day.

Her inability to continue was because the man whose privacy she was invading suddenly cut through her own defenses and for the first time in the experiment she perceived him as a human instead of an object. This ability to realize humanity in another individual is an extremely important key to how we act and react in body language as well as in all relationships. Dr. Sommer points out that an object, a non-person, cannot invade someone else's personal space, any more than a tree or a chair can. Nor is there any problem with invading the personal space of a non-person.

As an example Sommer cites the hospital nurses who discuss the patient's condition at his bedside, or the black maid in the white household who serves dinner while the guests debate the race question. Even the janitor who empties the waste basket in an office may not bother to knock when he enters, nor does the occupant of the office mind this intrusion. The janitor is not a real person to him. He's a non-person just as the man in the office is a non-person to the janitor.

Ceremonies and Seating

How we recognize and react to invasions includes a number of what Sommer calls "recognition ceremonies." In normal circumstances when you invade another's territory in either a library or a cafeteria, you send out a set of deferential signals. Verbally you apologize and ask, "Is this seat taken?" In body language you lower your eyes when you sit down.

When you take a seat on a crowded bus the proper ceremony is to keep your eyes straight ahead and avoid looking at the person sitting next to you. For other situations there are other ceremonies.

Defending personal space, according to Dr. Sommers, involves using the proper body language signals or gestures and postures as well as a choice of a location. How do you sit at an empty table when you wish to discourage other people from joining you? What body language do you use? A study by Sommers among university students showed that sitting down at an empty table when you wanted privacy usually involved use of two procedures. Either you look for privacy by positioning yourself as far as possible from other distracting people, or you attempt to get privacy by keeping the entire table to yourself alone.

If you look for privacy by retreating from others, you approach the problem from an avoidance viewpoint. You take a retreat position, usually at the corner of the table. In body language you say, "Share my table if you wish, but leave me alone. I am putting myself here at a corner so that the next person can sit as far from me as possible."

The other approach would be to try to keep the entire table to yourself. This is an offensive attitude and the aggressive person who chooses it would seat himself in the center of either side. He is saying, "Leave me alone. You cannot sit down without annoying me, so find another table!"

Among other findings of Dr. Sommer's study were the following: students who are in retreat, who wish to be as far away from others as they can get, will face away from the door. Students who wish to hog the entire table, who are in defense, will face the door. Most students, retreaters and defenders, preferred the back of the room, and most preferred small tables or tables against the wall.

In body language, students who sat squarely in the center of the table were asserting their dominance, their ability to handle the situation and also their desire to have the table to themselves.

The student who sat at the corner of the table signaled his wish to be left alone. "I don't mind if you share the table, but if you do, I have placed myself far away. You should do likewise. In that way we can both have our privacy."

The same is true of park benches. If you want privacy and you take a seat on an empty park bench you will most likely sit on the far end of either side indicating, "If you must sit here too, there is room enough to leave me alone."

If you don't want to share the bench you will position yourself in the center and communicate, "I want this bench as my own. Sit and you are intruding."

If you are willing to share your bench and your privacy then you will sit to one side, but not at the far end.

These approaches to the struggle for privacy reflect our inner personality. They indicate that the extroverted man will tend to go after his privacy by holding off the world. The introverted one will look for his by sharing his place with others, but keeping them at a distance. In both cases the body language involved includes a different set of signals, not a signal of body movement, but rather a signal of placement. "I put myself here and by doing so I say, 'Keep off' or "Sit here but do not intrude'."

This is similar to the signal transmitted by arranging the

body in various postures relating to the environment: behind the desk in an office, to signal, "Keep off, I am to be respected"; at the top of a judge's bench, the highest point in a courtroom, to signal, "I am far above you and therefore my judgement is best"; or close to someone else, violating their zone, to say, "You have no rights of your own. I move in on you at will and therefore I am superior."

5
The Masks
Men Wear

The Smile that Hides the Soul

There are many methods with which we defend our personal zones of space, and one of these is masking. The face we present to the outer world is rarely our real face. It is considered exceptional, almost peculiar behavior to show what we really feel in our facial expressions or in our actions. Instead we practice a careful discipline when it comes to the expression of our faces and bodies. Dr. Erving Goffman, in his book, *Behavior in Public Places*, states that one of the most obvious evidences of this discipline is the way we manage our personal appearance, the clothes we select and the hairdos we affect.

These carry a body language message to our friends and associates. Dr. Goffman believes that in public places the standard man of our society is expected to be neatly dressed and clean-shaven, with his hair combed and his hands and face clean. His study, written six years ago, didn't take into account the long hair, unshaven and careless or freer look of today's young people, a look that is slowly gaining acceptance. But this look too is one that is expected or formalized. It conforms to a general ideal.

Dr. Goffman makes the point that there are times, such as during the subway rush hour, when the careful masks we wear slip a bit, and "in a kind of temporary, uncaring, righteous exhaustion," we show ourselves as we really are. We let the defenses down and out of weariness or exasperation we forget to discipline our faces. Play the game of looking about a crowded bus, subway, or train during the rush hour after a day's work. See how much of the bare human being is allowed to show in all the faces.

Day after day we cover up this bare human being. We hold ourselves in careful control lest our bodies cry out messages our minds are too careless to hide. We smile constantly, for a smile is a sign not only of humor or pleasure but it is also an apology, a sign of defense or even an excuse.

I sit down next to you in a crowded restaurant. A weak smile says, "I don't mean to intrude, but this is the only vacant place."

I brush against you in a packed elevator and my smile says, "I am not really being aggressive, but forgive me anyway."

I am thrown against someone in a bus by a sudden stop, and my smile says, "I did not intend to hurt you. I beg your pardon."

And so we smile our way through the day, though in fact we may feel angry and annoyed beneath the smile. In business we smile at customers, at our bosses, at our employees; we smile at our children, at our neighbors, at our husbands and wives and relatives, and very few of our smiles have any real significance. They are simply the masks we wear.

The masking process goes beyond the facial muscles. We mask with our entire body. Women learn to sit in a certain way to conceal their sexuality, especially when their skirts are short. Men wear underwear that often binds their sexual organs. Women wear brassieres to keep their breasts in place and mask too much sexuality. We hold ourselves upright and button our shirts, zip up our flies, hold in our stomachs with muscle and girdle, and practice a variety of facial maskings. We have our party faces, our campus faces, our funeral faces and even in prison we have particular faces to wear.

In a book called *Prison Etiquette*, Dr. B. Phillips notes that new prisoners learn to "dogface," to wear an expression that is apathetic and characterless. When the prisoners are alone, however, in a reaction to the protective dogfacing of the day, they overreact and exaggerate their smiles, their laughter and the hate they feel toward their guards.

With advancing age the masks we use often become more difficult to wear. Certain women, who have relied on facial beauty all their lives, find it hard in the mornings of their old age to "get their faces together." The old man tends to forget himself and drools or lets his face go lax. With advancing age come tics, sagging jowls, frowns that won't relax and deep wrinkles that won't go away.

Take Off the Mask

Again, there are certain situations in which the mask drops. In a car, when our body zones are extended, we often feel free to drop the masks, and if someone cuts in front of us or tailgates us, we may loose tides of profanity that are shocking in their out-of-proportion emotions. Why do we feel so strongly in such minor situations? What great difference does it make if a car cuts us off or comes too close?

But here is a situation where we are generally invisible and the need to mask is gone. Our reactions can be all the greater because of this.

The dropping of the mask tells us a great deal about the need to wear a mask. In mental institutions the mask is often dropped. The mental patient, like the aging person, may neglect the most commonly accepted masks. Dr. Goffman tells of a woman in a ward for regressed females whose underwear was on wrong. She started, in full view of everybody, to adjust it by lifting her skirt, but when this didn't work she simply dropped her dress to the floor and fixed it, then pulled her dress up again quite calmly.

This attitude of ignoring the common devices of masking, such as clothes, of neglecting appearance and personal care, is often one of the most glaring signs of approaching psychotic behavior. Conversely, getting better in mental institutions is often equated with taking an interest in one's appearance.

Just as approaching psychotic behavior causes the patient to lose touch with reality and become confused in his verbal communication, causes him to say things that are divorced from reality, it also causes confusion in his body language. Here too he loses touch with the real world. He broadcasts statements that normal people keep hidden. He lets the inhibitions imposed by society slip, and he acts as if he were no longer conscious of an audience watching.

And yet this very loosening of body language may hold

the key to a greater understanding of the mentally disturbed patient. While a person can stop talking, the same person cannot stop communicating through his body language. He must say the right thing or the wrong thing, but he cannot say nothing. He can cut down on how much he communicates by body language if he acts in the proper fashion, or acts normally, the way people are supposed to act. In other words, if he behaves sanely, then he will send out the least amount of body language information.

But if he acts sanely, then of course he is sane. What other criteria do we have for sanity? So by definition, the insane man must act out his insanity and by so doing send a message to the world. This message, in the case of the mentally disturbed, is usually a cry for help. This puts an entirely new face on the strange actions of mentally disturbed people, and it opens up new avenues for therapy.

Masking cannot cover involuntary reactions. A tense situation may cause us to perspire, and there is no possible way to mask this. In another uncomfortable situation our hands may shake or our legs tremble. We can cover these lapses by putting our hands in our pockets, by sitting down to take the weight off our trembling legs, or by moving so quickly that the tremor isn't visible or noticed. Fear can be concealed by throwing yourself vigorously into the action you fear.

The Mask that Won't Come Off

The need to mask is often so deep that the process becomes self-perpetuating, and the mask cannot be taken off or let down. There are certain situations, such as sexual intercourse, where the masking should be stopped in order to enjoy love-making to its fullest, and yet many of us are only able to unmask in complete darkness. We are so afraid of what we may tell our partners by body language, or of what we may reveal with our faces, that we attempt to cut off the visual end of sex completely and we raise moral bulwarks to help us do this. "It's not decent to look." "The sexual organs are ugly." "A nice girl doesn't do that by daylight." And so on.

For many other people darkness is not enough to allow unmasking. Even in the dark they cannot drop the shields they have put up to protect themselves during sexual intercourse.

This, Dr. Goffman speculates, may be partly responsible for the large amounts of frigidity found in middle-class women. But in terms of sexual practice, Kinsey has shown that there are just as many shields, if not more, among the working classes. If anything, the middle class tends to be more experimental and less apt to shield its emotions.

The key to most masking in our society is often contained in books of etiquette. These will dictate what is proper and what isn't in terms of body language. One book suggests that it is wrong to rub our faces, touch our teeth or clean our fingernails in public. What to do with your body and your face when you meet friends or strangers is carefully spelled out by Emily Post. Her book of etiquette even describes how to ignore women. She discusses the "cut direct" and how to deliver it, "only with the gravest cause if you are a lady, and never to a lady if you are a man."

Part of our knowledge of masking is thus learned or absorbed from our culture, and part is taught specifically. But the technique of masking, though it is universal among mankind, varies from culture to culture. Certain aborigines, to be polite, must talk to each other without looking at each other's eyes, while in America it is polite to hold a partner's eyes while talking to him.

When Is a Person Not a Person

In any culture there are permissible moments when the mask may slip. Blacks in the South are well aware of the "hate stare" that a Southern white can give to them for no obvious reason except skin color. The same stare or naked show of hostility without masking can be given to another white by a white only under the greatest provocation and it is never permitted in America's Southern cultures to be given by a black to a white.

One of the reasons why the mask may be dropped, in this case, by the Southern white is because the Southern white sees the black as a non-person, an object not worth concerning himself about. In the South, however, the blacks have their own private signs. One black, by a certain signal of the eye, may tell another that he too is a brother, a black, even though his skin is so light that he could pass as a white. By another type of eye signal he may warn off a black and tell him, "I am passing as a white man."

Children, in our society, are treated as non-persons quite often and so are servants. We feel, perhaps consciously, perhaps unconsciously, that before these non-persons no mask is necessary. We cannot worry about hurting the feelings of a non-person. How can he have feelings to hurt?

This attitude is usually seen as a class-oriented thing. A class in society will apply it to the class beneath; higher-status people will apply it to lower-status people. The boss may not bother to mask in front of his employee, nor the lady in front of her maid any more than a father will mask in front of his child.

I sat in a restaurant recently with my wife, and a table away two dowager-type women were having cocktails. Everything about them from their furs to their hairdos cried out "wealth" and their bearing confirmed the fact. In the crowded restaurant they talked in voices so loud that they carried to every corner, yet their talk was private and intimate. The embarrassing result to the rest of the diners was that in order to maintain an illusion of privacy we all had either to pretend not to hear or to conduct ourselves and our own conversations so intently that we could block out the two dowagers.

In body language these two women were saying, "You are all of no real importance to us. You are all, in fact, not really people at all. You are non-persons. What we wish to do is all that matters, and so we cannot really embarrass anyone else."

Incidentally, instead of using their bodies to signal this message, these dowagers used voice volume, and it was not the intelligence of what they said but the amount of sound they used to say it that conveyed the message. Here we have the unusual technique of having two messages transmitted by one medium, the meaning of the words transmits one message, and the loudness of the voice transmits another.

These are cases where the mask is dropped but the dropping is almost contemptuous. Unmasking in front of a non-person is often no unmasking at all. In most cases we keep our masks on and the reason we keep them on is important. It is often dangerous in one way or another to unmask. When we are approached by a beggar in the street, if we do not wish to give him anything, it is important that we pretend he is not there and we have not seen him. We firm up the mask, look away and hurry past. If we were to allow ourselves to unmask in order to see the beggar as an individual not only would we have to face our own consciences, but we would also leave ourselves open to his importuning, pleading and possible attempt to embarrass us.

The same is true of many chance encounters. We cannot afford the time involved to exchange words and pleasantries, at least in urban areas. There are just too many people around us. In the suburbs or in the country it is different, and there is correspondingly less masking.

Also, by showing our real selves, we open ourselves to unpleasant interpretation. Dr. Goffman makes this clear in the setting of a mental institution. He describes a middle-aged man, a mental patient, who walked about with a folded newspaper and a rolled umbrella, wearing an expression of being late for an appointment. Keeping up the front that he was a normal businessman was overwhelmingly important to this patient, though in point of fact he was deceiving no one but himself.

In Eastern countries the masking procedure may be a physical one. The custom of women wearing veils is primarily to allow them to conceal their true emotions and so protect them from any male aggression. In these countries body language is so well recognized that it becomes an accepted fact that a man, with the slightest encouragement, will try to force sexual intercourse upon a woman. The veil allows the woman to hide her lower face and any unintentionally encouraging gesture. In the seventeenth century women used fans and masks on sticks for the same purpose.

The Masochist and the Sadist

In many cases masking can be used as an instrument of psychological torture. Take the case of Annie, married to Ralph, an older man, older and better educated and very conscious of the fact that Annie, intellectually and socially, was not his equal. Yet in a strange and somewhat perverted way Ralph loved Annie and realized she was the best wife for him. This did not prevent him from playing his own type of game with Annie, a game that involved masking to an intricate and exact degree.

When Ralph came home from work each day there was a well-standardized ritual. Annie must have his supper ready and waiting at exactly six-thirty, neither later nor earlier. He would arrive home at six, wash and read the afternoon paper until six-thirty. Then Annie would call him to the table and take her seat, watching his face furtively. Ralph knew she was watching him. She realized that he knew. But neither admitted to this.

Ralph would in no way indicate that the meal was either good or bad and as they ate Annie would construct a soap opera in her head. She would feel a sick despair in the pit of her stomach. Does Ralph like the food or doesn't he? If he doesn't, she knows what to expect: a cold upbraiding and a silent, miserable evening.

Annie would eat uneasily, watching Ralph's impassive face. Did she prepare the dish correctly? Did she season it properly? She followed the recipe, but she added some spices of her own. Was that a mistake? Yes, it must have been! She would feel her heart sink, her whole body tighten with misery. No, Ralph doesn't like it. Isn't his lip twisting in the beginning of a sneer?

Ralph, living the same soap opera, would look and for a long moment keep his face inscrutable while Annie would die a thousand deaths, and then he would smile his approval. And suddenly, miraculously, Annie's entire being would sing with happiness. Life is wonderful, and Ralph is her love and she is terribly, terribly happy. She would go back to her meal, enjoying the food now, ravenously hungry and delightfully pleased.

By careful manipulation of his mask, by timing his body language, Ralph has contrived a delicate torture and reward. He uses the same technique at night when he and Annie are in bed. He gives her no hint or indication of what he feels, of whether he will make love to her or not, and Annie goes through the same elaborate game of "Will he touch me? Does he still love me? How will I stand it if he rejects me!"

When finally Ralph does reach over and touch her Annie explodes in passionate ecstasy. Now the question of whether Annie is a victim or an accomplice is not for us to decide. The use of a mask to achieve the torture is the point to consider. The sado-masochist relationship of Annie and Ralph benefits both of them in a strange way, but for most mask-wearers the benefits of wearing the mask are more realistic.

How to Drop the Mask

The benefits of masking, real or imagined, make us reluctant to drop the mask. We might, among other things, be forcing a relationship other people do not want. Or we might risk being rejected. Yet the very wearing of the mask can cheat us of relationships we want. Do we gain as much as we lose?

Take the case of Claudia. In her early thirties, Claudia is attractive in a thin, intense way. Because of her job in a large investment firm Claudia comes in contact with many men during the course of her day, and she dates a great deal. But she is still single and, though she hates to admit it, still a virgin.

It's not for want of desire, Claudia insists. She is a passionate girl and looks ahead with horror to the prospect of a sterile old maid's life. Why then can't she become involved with a man emotionally and sexually? Claudia doesn't understand why, but the men she dates can.

"She turns you off," one of them explained. "Hell, I like Claudia. At work she's a great gal and I've taken her out, but the moment something begins to develop she freezes up and the message is very clear. Don't touch. I'm not having any. Who needs that?"

Who indeed? Who can see past Claudia's forbidding façade to the warm and passionate woman underneath? Claudia, in terror of rejection, does the rejecting first before anything can develop. In that way she's never hurt. She's never refused because she does the refusing first.

Stupid? Perhaps, but effective if being rejected is the worst thing in the world that can happen to you. For Claudia it is. So rather than take a chance she'll live out her days in loneliness.

Claudia's masking is unnecessary and wasteful, but there are necessary maskings decreed by the society. The person who masks according to this rule may desperately want to use body language to communicate, but isn't allowed to by custom.

An example of this masking is a nubile young friend, a girl of seventeen, who came to my wife with her problem.

"There's this boy I ride home with on the bus every day, and he gets off at my stop and I don't know him, but he's cute and I'd like to know him, and I think he likes me, but how can I get to be friendly?"

My wife, out of the wisdom of experience, suggested a couple of awkward, heavy packages for the next bus ride plus a carefully rehearsed stumble to send all the packages flying as she left the bus.

To my amazement it worked. The accident called forth the only possible response, since they were the only two passengers who left the bus at that stop. He helped her with the packages, and she was obliged to drop the mask. He, too, could now unmask, and by the time they reached her house she was able to ask him in for a Coke, and so it went.

At the proper time, then, the mask should often be dropped, must indeed be dropped if the individual is to grow and develop, if any meaningful relationship is to come about. The big problem with all of us is that after wearing a mask for a lifetime it is not so easy to drop it.

Sometimes the mask can only be dropped when further masking takes place. The man who dresses up in a clown suit for some amateur theatrical project often sheds his inhibitions as he dons his costume, and he is able to cavort and joke and "clown around" with perfect looseness and freedom.

The masking of darkness allows some of us the freedom to make love without masks, and for others the mask of anonymity serves the same purpose.

I have had male homosexuals tell me that they have had encounters with men, complete from pickup to sexual satisfaction, without even divulging their own names or learning their partners' names. When I asked how they could be so intimate without ever knowing their partners' names, the answer was invariably, "But that adds something to it. I can be relaxed and do what I want to. After all, we didn't know each other, and who cares what we did or said?"

To an extent, the same is true when a man visits a prostitute. The same anonymity may hold and bring with it a greater freedom.

But these are simply cases of double masking, of putting up another defense so that one may drop the mask. Along with the constant need to guard our body language, to keep a tight reign on the signals we send out, there is also a paradoxical need to transmit wildly and freely, to tell the world who we are and what we want, to cry out in the wilderness and be answered, to drop the mask and see if the hidden person is a being in his own right, in short, to free ourselves and to communicate.

6

The Wonderful World of Touch

Come Hold My Hand

Some time ago I volunteered to teach a young people's creative writing class at our local church. Harold, one of the young men who attended the class, was fourteen and a born troublemaker. Handsome, big for his age and very vocal, Harold made enemies without even trying, though usually he tried.

By the fifth session everyone hated him and he was well on his way to breaking up the group. For my part I was desperate. I tried everything from kindness and friendliness to anger and discipline, but nothing worked and Harold remained a sullen, disruptive force.

Then one evening he went a little too far in teasing one of the girls, and I grabbed him with both hands. The moment I did it, I realized my mistake. What could I do now? Let him go? Then he would be the victor. Hit him? Hardly, with the difference in age and size.

In a flash of inspiration I wrestled him to the ground and started to tickle him. He squealed with anger at first and then with laughter. Only when he gaspingly promised to behave did I let him up and found, to my own mixed reactions, that I had created a Frankenstein-type of monster. By tickling him I had invaded his body zone and prevented him from using it for defense.

Harold behaved himself from that time on, but Harold also became my devoted companion and buddy, hanging on my arm or my neck, pushing me or pummeling me and getting as close to me, physically, as he could.

I returned the closeness, and somehow we both made it through the session. What fascinated me was that by invading his personal sphere, by violating the sanctity of his territory, I had communicated with him for the first time.

What I learned from this encounter was that there are times when the masks must come down and communication must be by physical touch. We cannot achieve emotional freedom in many cases unless we can reach through our personal space, through the masks we set up as protection, to touch and fondle and interact physically with other people. Freedom perhaps is not an individual thing but a group function.

An awareness of this fact has led a group of psychologists to the formation of a new school of therapy, a school based very much on body language, but also concerned with breaking through the masking process by body contact.

The Crippling Masks

Children, before they are taught the inhibitions of our society, explore their world by touch. They touch their parents and cuddle into their arms, touch themselves, find joy in their genitals, security in the texture of their blankets, excitement in feeling cold things, hot things, smooth things and scratchy things.

But as the child grows up, his sense of awareness through touch is curtailed. The tactile world is narrowed. He learns to erect body shields, becomes aware of his territorial needs in terms of his culture, and discovers that masking may keep him from being hurt even though it also keeps him from experiencing direct emotions. He comes to believe that what he loses in expression, he gains in protection.

Unfortunately, as the child grows into adulthood, the masks all too often harden and tighten and change from protective devices to crippling devices. The adult may find that while the mask helps him to keep his privacy and prevents any unwanted relationship, it also becomes a limiting thing and prevents the relationships he wants as well as those he doesn't want.

Then the adult becomes mentally immobilized. But because mental qualities are easily translated into physical qualities, he becomes physically immobilized as well. The new therapy based on the experiments at the Esalen Institute at Big Sur in California, on research done among isolated groups of men living in Antarctica, and on group seminars all over the world called encounter groups, seeks to break through these physical immobilizations and work backward to the mental immobilization.

Dr. William C. Schutz has written a great deal about the new technique of encounter groups, a technique for preserving man's identity in the pressure of today's society. To show how much of feeling and behaving are expressed in body language, Dr. Schutz cites a number of interesting expressions that describe behavior and emotional states in body terms. Among these are: shoulder a burden; face up; chin up; grit your teeth; a stiff upper lip; bare your teeth; catch your eye; shrug it off; and so on.

The interesting thing about these is that they are all also body language phrases. Each of them expresses an emotion, but also expresses a physical body act that signals the same emotion.

When we consider these phrases we can understand Dr. Schutz's suggestion that "psychological attitudes affect body posture and functioning." He cites Dr. Ida Rolf's speculation that emotions harden the body in set patterns. The man who is constantly unhappy develops a frown as a set part of his physical being. The aggressive man who thrusts his head forward all the time develops a posture with head thrust forward and he cannot change it. His emotions, according to Dr. Rolf, cause his posture or expression to freeze into a given position. In turn, this position pulls the emotions into line. If you have a face frozen in a habitual smile, Dr. Rolf believes it will affect your personality and cause you to smile mentally. The same is true for a frown and for deeper, less obvious body postures.

Dr. Alexander Lowen, in his book *Physical Dynamics of Character Structure,* adds to this fascinating concept by stating that all neurotic problems are shown by the structure and function of the body. "No words are so clear as the language of body expression once one has learned to read it," he says.

He goes on to relate body function to emotion. A person with a sway back, he believes, can't have the strong ego of a man with a straight back. The straight back, on the other hand, is less flexible.

You Are What You Feel

Perhaps it is the knowledge of this linking of posture to emotion that makes an army direct its soldiers to stand straight and stiff. The hope is that eventually they will become immovable and determined. Certainly the cliché of the old soldier with the "ramrod up his back" and a rigid personality to go with it has some truth.

Lowen feels that retracted shoulders represent suppressed anger, raised shoulders are related to fear, square shoulders indicate shouldering responsibility, bowed shoulders carrying a burden, the weight of a heavy load.

It is difficult to separate fact from literary fancy in many of these suggestions of Lowen's, especially when he states that the bearing of the head is a function of ego strength and quality. He speaks of a long, proud neck or a short, bull neck.

Nevertheless there seems a great deal of sense in Lowen's relation of emotional states to their physical manifestations. If the way in which a person walks, sits, stands, moves, if his body language, indicates his mood and personality and ability to reach others, then there must be ways of causing a person to change by changing his body language.

Schutz, in his book *Joy*, notes that groups of people often sit with arms and legs crossed to indicate tightness and withdrawal, resistance against anyone else reaching them. Asking such a person to unlock himself, uncross his legs or arms, Schutz believes, will also open this person to communication with the rest of the group. The important thing is to know what the person is saying with his crossed arms and legs, what message he is sending. It is also important for the person himself to know what message he intends. He must be aware of the reasons for his own tension before he can break it.

How to Break Out of a Shell

How do you break out of your shell? How do you reach out to others? The first step in breaking free must be understanding that shell, understanding the defenses you have set up. Recently, at a counselor training center at New York University, I was shown a number of videotapes of interviews between counselors who were learning the counseling technique and troubled children who were being counseled.

In one tape, a pleasant-featured, well-dressed white woman who reeked of gentility was interviewing a disturbed and extremely introverted black girl of fourteen. The girl sat at a table with her head down, her face hidden from the woman, her left hand further covering her eyes and her right hand stretched across the table top.

As the interview progressed, the girl's left hand still shielded her eyes. She would not look up though she was quite articulate, but her right hand stole out across the table top toward the counselor, the fingers walking the hand along, retreating then advancing, cajoling and inviting, crying with an almost audible shriek of body language, "Touch me! For heaven's sake—touch me! Take my hand and force me to look at you!"

The white counselor, inexperienced in counseling techniques and thoroughly frightened by the entire experience, one of her first interviews, sat upright with her legs crossed and her arms folded across her chest. She smoked and moved only when she needed to tap the ash of her cigarette, but then her hand came back defensively across her chest. As plain as sight her physical attitude mirrored her mental attitude. "I am frightened and I cannot touch you. I don't know how to handle the situation, but I must protect myself."

How do you unlock such a situation?

Dr. Arnold Buchheimer, professor of education at the university, explained that the first step in unlocking came through showing the videotape (taken without the knowledge of either the counselor or the counselee) to the counselor. Along with this went an in-depth discussion of how she had reacted and why. She would then be encouraged to examine her own fears and hesitations, her own rigidity and tightness, and to attempt at the next session to achieve physical contact with the girl first and then verbal contact.

Before the series of counselor sessions was over, the counselor by training and analyzing her own behavior was able not only to reach the core of the girl's trouble on a verbal level, but also on a physical level; she was able to put her arm around her, hug her and give her some of the mothering she needed.

Her physical reaction was the first step toward opening a verbal reaction, and in due course toward helping the girl to help herself. In this situation the girl had asked in obvious body language for some physical contact. Her head down and her hand covering her eyes had said, "I am ashamed. I cannot face you. I am afraid." Her other hand, reaching across the table, said, "Touch me. Reassure me. Make contact with me."

The counselor by clasping her arms across her breast and sitting rigidly had said, "I am afraid, I cannot touch you nor permit you to invade my privacy."

Only when a mutual invasion became possible and there was direct physical contact could these two meet, then give and receive help.

The contact or invasion of privacy necessary to break down the barriers and strip away the masking need not always be physical. It can also be verbal. At a recent trip to Chicago I met a remarkable young man who was staying at my hotel. He had the unusual ability of verbally demolishing people's masks and barriers. Walking along the street with him one evening, we passed a restaurant in the style of the mid-nineteenth century. The doorman was dressed in a costume suitable to the period and physically was an imposing man.

My new friend stopped and to my intense embarrassment began the most intimate conversation with the doorman, intimate in terms of his family, his hopes in life and his achievements. To me it seemed the worst breach of good taste. One just does not intrude on a man's privacy in this way.

I was sure the reaction of the doorman would be to take offense, to be embarrassed and to withdraw. To my amazement, it was none of these. The doorman responded after only a moment's hesitancy, and before ten minutes were up, he had confided his hopes, ambitions and problems to my friend. We left him delighted and enthusiastic. Stunned, I asked my new friend, "Do you always come on that strong?"

"Why not?" he asked. "I care about that man. I was willing to ask about his problems and give him advice. He appreciated that. I feel better for doing it, and he feels better for my having done it."

The Silent Cocktail Party

It was true, but the ability to cut across the lines of taste and privacy is a rare thing. Not all of us have it, and not all of those who have it can avoid giving offense. I wonder too if my friend would have been as successful with someone who was his superior. Doormen are seen by many of us as non-persons and may react with gratitude to any notice.

But even if we cannot reach out verbally, we can devise methods of reaching each other in nonverbal ways, ways that may or may not include physical contact. One very successful way was a cocktail party given recently by a psychologist friend. He invited his guests with little invitations that informed them this was to be a nonverbal gathering.

"Touch, smell, stare and taste," his invitation read, "but don't speak. We're spending an evening in nonverbal communication."

My wife and I groaned at the precious quality of the invitation, but we couldn't gracefully get out of it. We went and to our surprise found it fascinating.

The room had been rearranged so that there were no available seats. We all stood and milled around, danced, gestured, mimed and went through elaborate charades, all without talking.

We knew only one other couple, and all our introductions were self-made and handicapped, or helped, by the imposed silence. We had to really work at getting to know each other, and amazingly enough we ended the evening with a clear and deep knowledge of our new friends.

What happened of course was that the verbal element of masking was taken away. All the rest of our masks were only half supported. They slipped easily and we found that we had to do without them to make our best contacts, and the contacts were physical for the most part.

In the silence, all accents and speech inflections and their link to status were eliminated. I shook hands with one man and noticed the callouses on his palm. This led to an acted-out version of his job with a construction crew and, without the barrier of words, to a closer understanding than is usually possible between two men in different class situations.

This is very much a parlor game, but a parlor game with a difference. There are no losers, and the total result is a more meaningful understanding of the people with whom you play. There are other games designed to enhance communication, to make body language understandable and to break down the barriers we erect to protect ourselves.

Playing Games for Health's Sake

Dr. Schutz has put together a number of these "parlor games," some garnered from the California Institute of Technology, some from the UCLA School of Business and some from the National Training Laboratories at Bethel, Maine. They are all designed to break down barriers, to unmask yourself and others and to make you aware of body language and its message.

One of them Schutz calls "Feeling Space." He instructs a group of people to sit together on the floor or in chairs and, with eyes closed, stretch out their hands and "feel" the space around them. Inevitably they will contact each other, touch and explore each other and react to that contact and their neighbor's intrusion upon their own bodies.

Some people, he notes, like to touch others and some do not. Some like being touched and some do not. The possible interactions, combinations, and permutations will often bring hidden emotions to the surface. If these are discussed afterward, the touchers and touchees can find a new awareness of themselves and their neighbors.

Another game Schutz calls "Blind Milling." Here, again with eyes closed, the group moves around a room encountering, touching and exploring each other with their hands. The end result is similar to that in Feeling Space.

Beyond these tentative explorations, Schutz suggests techniques that put emotional feeling into body language. As an example, he tells of a young man who withdrew from any direct relationship that might hurt him. It was easier for him to run away than to risk being hurt. To make him aware of what he was actually doing, his therapy group tried to get him to tell the person he disliked most in the group his true feelings about him. When he protested that he just could not do this, he was told to leave the group and sit in a corner. The physical acting out of his usual withdrawal made him realize he would rather withdraw than face a person directly and truthfully. He would rather remove himself from a group than risk doing something that might end up in an unpleasant situation, that might make someone else dislike him.

Much of the technique of the encounter groups is based on the physical acting out of an emotional problem.

On another level it is putting into body language what has already existed in emotional terms. Saying it with your body, however, allows you to understand it more completely.

In Schutz's technique, the man who has a suppressed hatred mixed with a very real love for his father, can best realize and deal with these conflicting emotions by pretending some other malleable object, say a pillow, is his father. He is encouraged to hit the pillow while expressing his anger and rage.

Often the furious beating of the pillow (if it does not come apart and fill the air with feathers) will carry the beater into an emotional state where his hostility to his father can empty out of him. Having expressed himself this way, in blatant physical terms, he may no longer feel in deep conflict, may indeed be able to express his love for his father, a love that has always been smothered by resentment and hostility.

What has happened to him is a freeing of emotion and the ability to hate as well as love. Often, instead of an inanimate object such as a pillow, the emotions can be freed in interaction between actual people.

Another technique for exposing a man to himself is for a group of people to form a circle with closed arms and let the person who is struggling to understand himself fight his way into the circle. The way in which he handles himself in this situation can help him to understand his real self and his real needs.

Some people will force and butt their way in to become part of a circle. Some will talk their way in, and others will use sly and devious techniques, such as tickling one member of the circle till he moves aside and lets the tickler join.

When a new encounter group is being formed, one interesting technique, Schutz suggests, is to have the members, one by one, brought up before the group to be examined physically, to be prodded, pushed, watched, touched and smelled. This he feels makes the reality of the person much greater to his fellow group members.

I would suggest that another technique could be based on

body language. One member of a group could be watched by the others and then described in terms of body language. What is he saying by his walk, by his stance, by his gestures? Is what we think he is saying the same as what he is actually saying?

A discussion of the signals sent and the signals received might enable a person to gain new insights. What messages do you send? Does your walk express the way you really feel, the way you think you feel, or the way others see you? We send out certain signals of body language and it is possible to learn more about ourselves by listening to others interpret the signals that we send.

Psychologists have been aware of this for a long time, and the technique of filming a man in a relationship with others, then showing the film to him and discussing his own signals, his own body language, has proved effective in opening his eyes to reality.

Without the sophisticated techniques of film and videotape, how can we begin to understand our own signals? There are a number of ways, and perhaps the most obvious and the easiest is through a parlor game like charades—but different.

One man or woman at a gathering or group goes out of the room and then enters and without words tries to get across an idea or an emotion such as happiness, ecstasy, mourning or chagrin. Without resorting to the symbolic gestures and abbreviations of charades, this becomes a problem of personality projection. The one trying to project the idea suddenly becomes aware of himself, of his own gestures and signals, of how he holds himself and how he moves.

Afterward, when the group discusses the success or failure of his attempt to speak with body language, he becomes aware of their reaction to his signals. Has he tried to signal shyness and succeeded instead in getting haughtiness across? Has he sent out amusement for pain, assurance for uncertainty? In the larger mirror of life itself does he also confuse his signals? Or are his signals correctly interpreted?

This is a matter we should all take some time to consider. Do we present our real selves to the world? Are the messages our friends receive the same as the ones we think we send? If they aren't, this may be part of our failure to integrate into the world. This may be a clue toward understanding our failures in life.

Another parlor game that can help toward self-understanding is to ask a group to give one of its members a new name, a name that is suited to his body movements. Then the person is asked to act in accordance with the new name the group has given him. Often the sudden freedom to act in a new fashion, to accept a new personality, will serve as a liberating force and will clear away inhibitions, allowing the newly named person to understand himself on a different level. This is acting out a new personality, but also a personality he would prefer to the one he has.

There are other variations of "acting out" that can cut to the heart of a situation. A friend of mine told me recently that in his own family he was having some very serious problems between his seventeen-year-old daughter and his fourteen-year-old son. "They've gotten to the stage where they can't be in the same room without exploding. Everything he does is wrong in her eyes, and she's always at him."

At my suggestion he tried a nonverbal game with the two of them and told them to do whatever they wanted, but not to use words.

"For a few moments," he told me later, "they were at a

loss. Without words she couldn't scold him, and it seemed as if she didn't know what else to do, what other way to relate to him. Then he came over to where she was sitting and grinned at her, and all at once she caught him, pulled him down on her lap and actually cuddled him to the amazement of the rest of the family."

What came out of this in a discussion later was that the entire family agreed that by her actions she had seemed to be mothering him. She did indeed feel like a mother to him, and her constant scolding was less in the nature of criticism and more in the nature of possessive mother-love. Her body language action of cuddling made her aware of this and opened his eyes as well. Afterward, my friend reported, while they continued their bickering, it was hardly as serious as before and underlying it on both parts was a new warmth and understanding.

What often happens in any relationship is that language itself becomes a mask and a means of clouding and confusing the relationship. If the spoken language is stripped away and the only communication left is body language, the truth will find some way of poking through. Spoken language itself is a great obscurer.

In love and in sexual encounters, the spoken word can act as a deterrent to the truth. One of the most useful therapeutic exercises for a couple in love is to attempt, in complete darkness, to transmit a definite message to each other with only the tactile elements of body language. Try to tell your lover: "I need you. I will make you happy." Or "I resent you. You do not do this or that properly." "You are too demanding." "You are not demanding enough."

Stripped of words, these exercises in sexuality and love can become intensely meaningful and can help a relationship develop and grow. The same communication without words, but with the visual instead of the tactile sense, can be a second step in the maturing of a love affair. Somehow it is a great deal easier for many people to look at each other's bodies after having touched them.

7

The Silent Language of Love

Stance, Glance and Advance

Mike is a ladies' man, someone who is never at a loss for a girl. Mike can enter a party full of strangers and within ten minutes end up on intimate terms with one of the girls. Within half an hour he has cut her out of the pack and is on his way home with her—to his or her place, depending on which is closer.

How does Mike do it? Other men who have spent half the evening drumming up enough courage to approach a girl, will see Mike come in and take over quickly and effectively. But they don't know why.

Ask the girls and they'll shrug. "I don't know. He just has his antennae out, I guess. I get signals, and I answer them, and the first thing I know. . . ."

Mike is not particularly good looking. He's smart enough,

94

but that's not his attraction. It seems that Mike almost has a sixth sense about him. If there's an available girl Mike will find her, or she will find him.

What does Mike have?

Well, if he hasn't looks or brilliance, he has something far more important for this type of encounter. Mike has an unconscious command of body language and he uses it expertly. When Mike saunters into a room he signals his message automatically. "I'm available, I'm masculine. I'm aggressive and knowledgeable." And then when he zeroes in on his chosen subject, the signals go, "I'm interested in you. You attract me. There's something exciting about you and I want to find out what it is."

Watch Mike in action. Watch him make contact and signal his availability. We all know at least one Mike, and we all envy him his ability. What is the body language he uses?

Well, Mike's appeal, Mike's nonverbal clarity, is compounded of many things. His appearance is part of it. Not the appearance he was born with, that's rather ordinary, but the way Mike has rearranged that appearance to transmit his message. There is, when you look at Mike carefully, a definite sexuality about him.

"Of course," a knowing woman will say, "Mike is a very sexy man." But sexy how? Not in his features.

Pressed further, the woman will explain, "It's something about him, something he has, a sort of aura."

Actually it's nothing of the sort, nothing so vague as an aura. In part it's the way Mike dresses, the type of pants he chooses, his shirts and jackets and ties, the way he combs his hair, the length of his sideburns—these all contribute to the immediate picture, but even more important than this is the way Mike stands and walks.

One woman described it as an "easy grace." A man who knew Mike was not so kind. "He's greasy." What came through as pleasing to the woman was transmitted as disturbing or challenging and therefore distasteful to the man, and he reacted by characterizing the quality contemptuously.

Yet Mike does move with grace, an arrogant sort of grace that could well arouse a man's envy and a woman's excitement. A few actors have that same movement, Paul Newman, Marlon Brando, Rip Torn, and with it they can transmit an obvious sexual message. The message can be broken down into the way they hold themselves, their stance or posture, and the easy confidence of their motion. The man who has that walk needs little else to turn a woman's head.

But Mike has more. He has dozens of little gestures, perhaps unconscious ones, that send out elaborations of his sexual message. When Mike leans up against a mantel in a room to look around at the women, his hips are thrust forward slightly, as if they were cantilevered, and his legs are usually apart. There is something in this stance that spells sex.

Watch Mike when he stands like this. He will lock his thumbs in his belt right above the pockets, and his fingers will point down toward his genitals. You have surely seen the same stance a hundred times in western movies, usually not taken by the hero, but by the sexy bad guy as he lounges against a corral fence, the picture of threatening sexuality, the villain the men hate and the women—well, what they feel is a lot more complex than hate or desire or fear, and yet it's a mixture of all these things. With his blatant body language, his leather chaps, his cantilevered groin and pointing fingers he is sending out a crude, obvious but effective signal. "I am a sexual threat. I am a dangerous man for a woman to be alone with. I am all man and I want you!"

On a minor scale, less blatant, Mike sends out the same message.

But his body language doesn't stop there. This much serves to signal his intentions, to create an atmosphere, an aura if you will. This fascinates the available women and interests or even irritates the non-available ones.

Mike himself explained how he proceeded after this. "I size up the women, the ones who want it. How? It's easy. By the way they stand or sit. And then I make my choice and I catch her eye. If she's interested she'll respond. If not, I forget her."

"How do you catch her eye?"

"I hold the glance a little longer than I should, since I don't really know her. I won't let her eyes slide away, and I narrow mine—sort of."

But there is even more to Mike's approach than the insistent eye, as I observed one evening at a party. Mike has an uncanny instinct for sizing up a woman's defensive body language and insistently breaking it down. Are her arms clasped defensively? He opens his. Is her posture rigid? He relaxes as they talk. Is her face pinched and drawn? He smiles and loosens his face.

In short, he answers her body signals with opposite and complementary signals of his own, and by doing this intrudes himself into her awareness. He brushes aside her body language pretenses, and because unconsciously she really wants to open herself up, she opens up to Mike.

Mike moves in on a woman. When he has made signal contact, when his body language gets the message of his availability across, his next step is physical invasion, but physical invasion without touch.

He cuts into the woman's territory or body zone. He comes close enough for her to be uneasy, and yet not close enough for her to logically object. Mike doesn't touch his victim needlessly. His closeness, his intrusion into her territory, is enough to change the situation between them.

Then Mike carries his invasion even further by visual intrusion as they talk. What they say really doesn't matter much. Mike's eyes do far more talking than his voice. They linger on the woman's throat, on her breasts, her body. They linger sensuously and with promise. Mike touches his tongue to his lips, narrows his eyes, and invariably the woman becomes uneasy and excited. Remember, she's not just any woman, but that particular susceptible woman who has responded to Mike's opening gambit. She has returned his flattering attentions, and now she is in too deep to protest.

And anyway, what could she protest against? Just what has Mike done? He hasn't touched her. He hasn't made any suggestive remark. He is, by all the standards of society, a perfect gentleman. If his eyes are a bit too hot, a bit too bold, this is still a matter of interpretation. If the girl doesn't like it she has only to be rude and move off.

But why shouldn't the girl like it? Mike is flattering her with his attention. In effect he is saying, "You interest me. I want to know you better, more intimately. You're not like other women. You're the only woman here I care about."

For, in addition to his flattering attention to this woman, Mike never makes the mistake of spreading his interest. He narrows his focus and speaks to only one woman, and he makes the impact of his body language all the stronger for it. Half the time, when Mike leaves with the girl of his choice, she hardly needs any persuasion. By that time a simple, "Let's go!" is enough.

Is She Available?

How does Mike single out his victim? What body language does an available girl at a party use to say, "I'm available. I'm interested. I can be had"? There must be a definite set of signals because Mike rarely makes a mistake.

A girl in our society has an additional problem in this game of sexual encounters. No matter how available she may be, it's considered pretty square to let anyone know it. This would instantly put her value down and cheapen her. And yet, unconsciously, she must let her intent be known. How does she do it?

A big part of the way she transmits her message is also in stance, posture or movement. An available woman moves in a studied way. A man may label it posing, another woman, affectation, but the movement of her body, hips and shoulders telegraph her availability. She may sit with her legs apart, symbolically open and inviting, or she may affect a gesture in which one hand touches her breast in a near caress. She may stroke her thighs as she talks or walk with a languorous roll to her hips. Some of her movements are studied and conscious, some completely unconscious.

A few generations ago female availability was broadly burlesqued by Mae West's "come up and see me sometime" routine. A later generation turned to the baby-face and hushed and breathless voice quality of a Marilyn Monroe—a tarnished innocence. Today, in a more cynical age, it is again blatant sexuality. Someone like Raquel Welch spells out the message. But these are the obvious, motion picture messages. On a subtler, living room level, the level on which Mike operates, the message is more discreet, often so discreet that the man who is ignorant of body language misses it completely. Even the man who knows a little about the subject may be misled. For example, the woman who crosses her arms across her chest may be transmitting the classic signal, "I am closed to any advance. I will not listen to you, or hear you."

This is a common interpretation of closed arms, and it is one with which most psychologists are familiar. As an example of this, there was a recent story in the papers about Dr. Spock addressing a class at the Police Academy. The audience of police were extremely hostile to the good doctor, in spite of the fact that he was responsible for the way most of them and their children had been brought up. They demonstrated their hostility verbally in their discussion, but also much more obviously in body language. In the news photo, every policeman sat with his arms crossed tightly over his chest, his face hard and closed.

Very clearly they were saying, "I am sitting here with a closed mind. No matter what you say I'm unwilling to listen. We just can't meet." This is the classical interpretation of crossed arms.

But there is another equally valid interpretation. Crossed arms may say, "I am frustrated. I am not getting what I need. I am closed in, locked in. Let me out. I can be approached and am readily available."

While the man who knows only a little about body language may misinterpret this gesture, the man well educated in body language will get the correct message from the accompanying signals the girl sends out. Is her face pinched

and tight with frustration? Is she sitting stiffly instead of in
a relaxed position? Does she avert her eye when you try to
catch it?

All the body signals must be added up to a correct total if
a man is to use body language effectively.

The aggressively available woman acts in a predictable
fashion too. She has a number of effective tricks of body language to telegraph her availability. As Mike does, she uses
territorial intrusion to make her point. She will sit uncom-
fortably close to the man she is after, taking advantage of
the uneasiness such closeness arouses. As the man shifts and
fidgets, unaware of why he is disturbed, she will move in
with other signals, using his uneasiness as a means of throwing him off balance.

While a man on the make cannot touch the woman if he
is to play the game fairly, it is perfectly permissible for a
woman on the make, at this stage of the game, to touch the
man. This touch can exaggerate the uneasiness of the man
into whose territory she has cut.

A touch on the arm can be a disarming blow. "Do you
have a match?" Steadying the hand that holds it to her cigarette can allow a moment of flesh-to-flesh contact that may
be effectively troubling.

The contact of a woman's thigh, or her hand carelessly
brushed against a man's thigh can be devastating if it is applied at just the right moment.

The aggressive approach by a woman can utilize not only
body language—the adjustment of a skirt as she sits close,
the uncrossing of her legs, the thrusting forward of her
breasts, a pouting mouth—it can also utilize smell. The right
perfume in the right amount, to give an elusive but exciting
scent, is an important part of the aggressive approach.

Is the Face Worth Saving?

But sight, touch and smell are still less than the complete arsenal of the woman on the warpath. Sound is a very definite part of the approach. It is not always what she says, but the tone of her voice, the invitation behind the words, the pitch and the intimate, caressing quality of the sound.

The French actresses understand this well, but French is a language that lends itself to sexuality, no matter what is being said. One of the most amusing off-Broadway revue sketches I have ever seen consisted of an actor and actress doing a "scene" from a French movie. Each recited a list of vegetables in French, but the tone of voice, cadence and vocal innuendo dripped sexuality.

This, as we described earlier in the book, is the use of one communication band to carry two messages. In the area of love and sex it is a very common use. For the aggressively available woman it can serve to throw a man off guard. This is a trick used by both men and woman in the aggressive sexual pursuit. If you throw your quarry off balance, make him or her uneasy, moving in for the kill becomes relatively easy.

The trick of using the voice to carry one innocuous spoken message and another more meaningful, and much stronger, unspoken message is particularly effective because the quarry, male or female, cannot protest by the rules of the game. The aggressor, if protest is made, can always draw back and say, with some truth, "But what did I do? What did I say?"

There is a face-saving device in this, for no matter how hot the pursuit of love or sex, it cannot be done with the risk of losing face. For many people, particularly if they are insecure, losing face is a devastating and humiliating occurrence. The sexual aggressor, if he or she is truly successful at the trade, is concerned with face-saving in his victim only as a means of manipulating his quarry. To be sexually aggressive, a man or woman must have enough self-assurance, enough security, to function without the need of face-saving devices.

On the opposite side of the coin, the sexually insecure person, the quarry in the inevitable hunt, desperately needs to avoid humiliation, to save face. This puts her at a tremendous disadvantage in the game. The aggressor can manipulate the quarry, holding loss of face as a threat.

When, for example, the aggressor moves in on the quarry's territory and, using a sexually seductive voice, speaks in obvious banalities, what is the quarry to do? Move back and risk the raised eyebrow. "What did you think I wanted?"

To assume that the aggressor is after *her* sexually is to import more worth to *herself* than *she* truly believes *she* has. To be let down after this would be too humiliating to bear. Suppose *she* were truly misinterpreting *his* motives? So, in most cases, the aggressor gets away with *his* ploy.

The same type of interaction is used by the deviate sexual aggressor outside of a social situation. The male subway-sexual deviate who attempts to fondle or touch a female rider in a crowd depends on her fright and insecurity to keep her quiet. The same dynamics are in action, and the fear of losing face may prevent her from protesting. She endures the minor annoyance of a groping pervert or an exposing pervert in order not to attract attention to herself.

This is so much an expected reaction that many sexual perverts who achieve satisfaction from exposing themselves count on the embarrassment and shame of their victims. Should the victim react by laughing or by any show of amusement, or even by aggressively approaching him, it would be a devastating experience for the deviate.

Pickups, AC and DC

On the theme of deviates, among both male homosexuals and lesbians there are definite body language signals that can establish intimate communication. Homosexuals "cruising" on a street can identify a sympathetic soul without exchanging a word.

"Making contact is relatively simple," a young homosexual recently explained in a survey. "The first thing to do is to identify your man, and it's hard to tell you how it's done, because there are so many little signals. Some of it is the way he walks, though many of us walk like perfectly normal men. Mostly, I guess, it's the eye contact. You look and you know. He holds your eye just a little too long, and then his eye may travel down your body. The quick glance to the crotch and away is a sure giveaway."

Discussing his own signals, he explains, "I walk past and then look back. If there's any interest he'll look back too. Then I slow down, stop to look at a store window. Then we'll drift back towards each other . . . and contact!"

The signals are rigid and formalized, and sometimes they are unspoken but on the verbal band, though not related to the words. Dr. Goffman tells of a homosexual who stopped into a "gay" bar for a drink but had no interest in picking anyone up. He took out a cigarette, but found he had no matches. He suddenly realized that to ask anyone at the bar for a match was the understood signal, "I am interested. Are you?"

In the end he bought a pack of matches from the bartender.

The homosexual's signals for initiating contact are not far divorced from the normal man's signals for picking up a girl. A long time ago, when I was a soldier on leave in Boston, a soldier friend cajoled me into coming out with him to "pick up some dames."

I had had no experience at this, but I had to play the "bigshot" since I couldn't admit my ignorance. I went along and watched my friend carefully. Within half an hour he had "picked up" five girls and selected two for us. His technique was built on body language.

Walking along the street, or more properly, sauntering along, he would catch a prospect's eye, hold it a bit longer than was necessary and lift one eyebrow. If the girl faltered in her stride, stopped to look at her compact, to fix her stockings or window-shop down the street, it was one of a number of return signals that meant, "I am aware of you and possibly interested. Let's pursue this further."

My friend would then break stride, turn and follow behind the girl for a block. The following without making contact was a necessary part of the ritual and allowed him to begin vocal contact, to comment to me, a third party, on her dress, her walk, her looks—all in semi-humorous terms, a face-saving device to avoid offense.

At first she would pretend his advances were unwelcome. If this stage lasted too long it would be mutually agreed that his advances really were unwelcome. If, however, she giggled or answered him, or commented on him to her girl friend, if she had one, then it indicated a growing interest.

Eventually the pickup ended with my friend side-by-side with the girl, talking her into an apparently reluctant familiarity. I have seen the very same technique used today among teen-agers and it is one in which every step is rigidly outlined and the game must be played out from start to finish. At any point negotiations can be easily broken off by either partner without loss of face to the other. This is a stringent requirement of a successful and smooth pickup.

There is something ritualistically similar to this in the opening ceremony of certain encounters among animal species. Watch two pigeons in the park as the male circles, pouts and goes through a formal pickup while the female pretends indifference. A very definite body language is in use and in the same way humans approach each other in courtship with definite body language.

Dr. Gerhard Nielsen of the Psychological Laboratory at the University of Copenhagen describes in his book, *Studies in Self-Confrontation*, the extremely important use of body language in what he calls the "courtship dance" of the American adolescent.

Breaking the procedure of courtship down to a cold, clinical level, Dr. Nielsen found twenty-four steps between the "initial contact between the young male and female and the coitional act." These steps by the man, he decided, and the counter steps taken by the girl had a "coercive order." He explains this by saying that when a boy takes the step of holding a girl's hand, he must wait until she presses his hand, signaling a go-ahead, before he can take the next step of allowing his fingers to intertwine with hers.

Step must follow step until he can casually put his arm around her shoulder. He may move his hand down her back then and approach her breast from the side. She, in turn, can block this approach with her upper arm against her side.

After the initial kiss, and only then, he may try to move toward her breast again, but he does not really expect to reach it until a good deal of kissing has taken place. Proto-col forbids him to approach the breast from the front, even as it forbids the first kiss before the initial hand-holding.

Dr. Neilsen suggests that the boy or girl is labeled "fast" or "slow" in terms of the order of each step, not the time taken for each step. "Skipping steps or reversing their order is fast," in the same way that ignoring the signal to move on to the next step, or not permitting the next step, is slow.

Choose Your Posture

Dr. Albert E. Scheflen, professor of psychiatry at the Albert Einstein College of Medicine in New York City, has studied and charted patterns of courtship and what he calls "quasi-courtship" in human beings. This quasi-courtship is the use of courting or flirting or sex to achieve non-sexual goals.

All human behavior is patterned and systematic, according to Dr. Scheflen, and it is also made up of regular, small segments arranged into larger units. This is equally true for sexual behavior, and in a study of the elements that make up our sexual relations to each other, Dr. Scheflen found that in business meetings, at parties, in school and in many other gatherings, people used these sexual elements, even though they had no sexual goal in mind.

He came to the conclusion that either Americans behave sexually when they get together on a non-sexual basis, or else—and more likely—the sexual behavior has certain qualifying body language signals when it is not used with the ultimate goal of sexual intercourse.

Just what are these sexual patterns of behavior? Well, according to Dr. Scheflen's investigations, when a man and a woman prepare for a sexual encounter, although they are unaware of what they are doing, they go through a number of body changes that bring them into a state of readiness.

The muscles of their bodies become slightly tensed and "ready for action." Body sagging disappears, and they stand up straighter, more erect and alert. There is less "jowling" in their faces and "bagging" around their eyes. Their posture becomes more youthful, and their stomachs are pulled in, their leg muscles tightened. Even their eyes seem brighter while their skins may blush or grow pale. There may even be changes in their body odors, harking back to a more primitive time when smell was a tremendously important sense in sexual encounters.

As these changes take place, the man or woman may begin to use certain gestures which Dr. Scheflen calls "preening behavior." A woman will stroke her hair or check her makeup, rearrange her clothes or push her hair away from her face, while a man may comb his hair, button his coat, readjust his clothes, pull up his socks, arrange his tie or straighten the crease in his trousers.

These are all body language signals that say, "I am interested. I like you. Notice me. I am an attractive man—an attractive woman. . . ."

The second step in these sexual encounters consists of positioning. Watch a man and a woman at a party, a couple who are getting to know one another and feel a mounting sexual interest in each other. How do they sit? They will arrange their bodies and heads to face one another. They will lean toward each other and try to block off any third person. They may do this by using their arms to close a circle, or by crossing their feet toward each other to block out anyone else.

Sometimes, if such a couple are sharing a sofa and a third person is on a facing chair, they will be torn between two compulsions. One is the desire to close in their own spaces, to include only themselves, and the other is the social responsibility of having to include the third person. They may solve their dilemma by having the best of both worlds. They may cross their legs to signal to each other that they are a closed circle. The one on the right will cross his right leg over his left. The one on the left will cross her left leg over her right. In effect this closes the two of them off from the third—from the waist down. However, social responsibility to the third person may make them arrange the top parts of their bodies directly facing him, thus opening themselves to him.

When one woman at a gathering wants to get a man into an intimate situation where the two of them can form a closed unit, she acts as the sexually aggressive woman does, but to a lesser degree. She utilizes body language that includes flirting glances, holding his eyes, putting her head to one side, rolling her hips, crossing her legs to reveal part of her thigh, putting a hand on her hip or exposing her wrist or palm. All of these are accepted signals that get a message across without words. "Come and sit near me. I find you attractive. I would like to know you better."

Now let us take a situation without sexual overtones. In a conference room at a big industrial firm, a male and a female executive discuss production costs with other officials. They may go through what appear to be these same sexual encounter signals. They are using body language that in other circumstances would invite sexual advances, and yet quite obviously these two have their minds entirely on the business matter in hand. Are they masking their true feelings and do they really have a sexual desire for each other? Or are we misinterpreting their body language?

In a college seminar it appears, to an uninitiated eye, that one of the girl students is using body language to send signals to the professor, signals that invite a sexual encounter. He in turn reacts as if he were agreeable. Are they in fact flirting, or are these really non-sexual signals? Or is there something wrong with our interpretation of body language?

A group psychotherapy seminar has a group therapist who uses body language to make "advances" to one of the women. Is he stepping out of line and violating his code of ethics? Or is this part of his therapy? Or again, are the signals confused?

After careful study of these and similar situations, Dr. Scheflen found that often sexual signals were sent out when the people involved had no intention of getting into any sexual encounter. However, he found that the body language signals sent out when a sexual encounter was expected as the end result of a meeting were not quite the same as those sent out for non-sexual endings. There were subtle differences that announced, "I am interested in you and I want to do business with you, but this is not a sexual matter."

Semi-Sexual Encounters

How do we make it clear to each other that the encounter is to be non-sexual? We do it by sending another sign along with the signal, a bit of body language over and above the obvious body language, another case of two signals on one communications band.

One method for letting a partner know that the sexual

signals are not to be taken seriously is to refer, in some way, to the fact that this is a business meeting, or a classroom, or a psychotherapy group. It could be something as simple as a gesture or a movement of the eyes or head toward someone in authority, or toward the other members of the gathering.

Another trick to separate sex from business is to make the sexual body language signal incomplete, to omit an important part of it. Two people sitting close together at a business meeting may adopt a sexual relationship by facing each other, but may turn part of their bodies away, or put their arms out to include others in their private circle. They may break partner contact with their eyes, or raise their voices to include everyone else in the room.

In each case a vital element must be missing from the sexual encounter. The missing element may be eye linkage, a low and private voice, arms arranged to include only the partner or any of a number of other intimacies.

Another way of putting the situation on a non-sexual level is to use disclaimers, to refer in talk to a wife, a boyfriend, a fiancée. This brings the situation into proper focus and tells the partner, "We are friends, not lovers."

This goes back to Dr. Scheflen's belief that behavior occurs in specified units that make up whole patterns. If some of the units are omitted, the finished pattern is different. In this case it is changed from sexual to non-sexual, but still with a strong man-woman interaction. A certain business routine takes place, but it is spiced by a strong flavor of half-teasing sexuality. The participants, without any expectation of sexual gratification, are still exploiting the fact that there is a sexual difference between them. The businessman uses sexual body language signals to get a certain relationship across. The intellectual uses it as a teaching aid, and the therapist uses it to help a psychological situation, but they are all aware that they are simply manipulating their genders, not aiming at sexual gratification.

There is, however, no guarantee that in any of these situations sexuality will not develop. There have been enough teachers responding sexually to pupils, businessmen to businesswomen and therapists to patients to give all of these encounters a certain piquancy and even promise.

These semi-sexual encounters occur so frequently that they are an innate part of our culture. Not only do they take place out of the home, but they also occur between parents and children, hosts and guests, even between two women or two men. The one thing that must always be made clear in this sexual-non-sexual relationship is that it is not for real. From the beginning the qualifications or disclaimers must be in effect. There should, if it is done properly, be no possibility of one partner suddenly waking up to say, "But I thought you meant . . ."; and of the other having to protest, "Oh no, it wasn't that way at all."

Dr. Scheflen notes that there are some psychotherapists who use this flirtation behavior very consciously to involve their patients. A disinterested female patient may be made to talk openly by a sexual approach on the part of her therapist, sexual of course in terms of body language. He may arrange his tie, his sock or his hair in a preening manner to transmit sexual interest, but he must, of course, make his true non-sexual position known.

Dr. Scheflen describes a situation of a family visiting a therapist, a mother, daughter, grandmother and father. Whenever the therapist would talk to the daughter or grandmother, the mother, who sat between them, would begin to transmit sexual signals in body language. This would serve to draw the therapist's attention back to her, a sort of flirting procedure that is very common among women when they are not the center of attention. She would pout, cross her legs and extend them, place her hand on her hips and lean her body forward.

When the therapist unconsciously responded to her "advances" by arranging his tie or hair or leaning forward, both the girl and the grandmother on either side of the mother would cross their legs, placing the crossed leg in front of the mother from either side and, in effect, "boxing her in." She, in turn, would stop her sexual signals and lean back.

Perhaps the most interesting thing about this entire charade was that the "boxing in" by daughter and grandmother was always done at a signal from the father. The signal—waving his crossed foot up and down! And all of this was done by therapist, women and father without any of them being aware of their own signaling.

From a careful study of sexual-non-sexual behavior, Scheflen concludes that it usually occurs between two people when one becomes preoccupied or turns away from the other for some reason. In a large group, a family, a business gathering or a classroom, it also happens when one member is ignored or excluded by the others. The excluded member may "preen" in a sexual way to get back into the group. When one member of a group withdraws it may also be used by the rest of the group to call him back.

The important part in all of this is to know the signals, to know the limiting or qualifying signals that separate real sexual advances from non-sexual. The two, Scheflen believes, are easily confused. Indeed there are people who regularly confuse both the sending and receiving of these sexual signals and their qualifiers. There are people who, for psychological reasons, cannot follow through a sexual encounter, but still act in a sexually seductive manner, particularly when they should not.

These people not only provoke sexual advances, but see such advances in others when no such advances are intended. This is the typical "tease" all of us know or the girl who is sure everyone has designs on her.

On the other hand, Scheflen lists those people who are not aware of the qualifying signals telling them that the advance is not really sexual. These people freeze up in ordinary non-sexual situations and withdraw.

How the body language for these situations is learned and how we know the correct interpretations, the correct disclaimers and qualifiers to make sexual advances non-sexual, how we learn all of this is hard to explain. Some is taught and some is absorbed from the culture. When, for one reason or another, an individual has been divorced from his society and hasn't been taught the proper interpretations of these signals, he may face a good deal of trouble. For him body language may be unknown on a conscious level and unused on an unconscious level.

8
Positions, Points and Postures

A Cry for Help

The patient was hardly more than a boy, seventeen years old, but he looked younger. He was pale and thin and he had a curious, uncertain quality to his face, as if someone had thought better about creating him and tried to erase his features but had only succeeded in smudging them. He was dressed carelessly and sloppily, and he sat in a listless way, his arms crossed, his eyes vague. When he moved, his motions were tight and restricted. When he came to rest he was slumped over and passive.

The therapist glanced at his watch surreptitiously, grateful that the hour was at an end, and he forced a smile. "That's all then, till tomorrow."

The boy stood up and shrugged. "What tomorrow? Don't you worry about tomorrow. I'm sure not going to after tonight. There won't be any tomorrow for me."

At the door the therapist said, "Now come on, Don.

You've threatened suicide every week for the past six months."

The boy looked at him dully and then left, and the therapist stood watching the door uncertainly. Don was his last patient for the day, and he should have felt relieved. Instead he was filled with an uneasiness that steadily grew worse. He tried to work at his records for awhile, but he couldn't. Something bothered him, something about the boy. Was it the way he talked, his threat of suicide? But he had threatened to kill himself before, many times. Why was this threat any different?

Why was he disturbed now? He remembered his uneasy feeling during the session, how passive the boy had been. He recalled his gestures, the limited range of motion when he moved, his inability to hold his eye.

Uneasily the therapist cast back over the hour. Somehow, in some way, he had become convinced that this time was different, that this time the boy meant suicide. Yet what had he said that was different? What had he said that he hadn't said in every other session?

The therapist went to the console with the concealed tape recorder, his way of preserving each session, and he played back the tape of the past hour. Nowhere in any of the boy's words was there a hint of anything different or unusual, but the tone of voice was flat, lifeless, passive.

His uneasiness grew. Somehow a message had come across during the session. He had to trust that message even without knowing what it was. Finally, half annoyed at himself and yet half relieved, he called his wife and said he'd be home late and then set out for the boy's home.

The rest of the story is simple and direct. The therapist was right. The boy had attempted suicide. He had gone straight home, taken a bottle of pills from the family's medicine cabinet and locked himself in his room. Fortunately the therapist was in time. The parents were readily convinced, and the family physician was able to clean out the boy's stomach with an emetic. The bright lining to the cloud was that this event became the turning point in the boy's therapy. Progress was all uphill after that.

"But why?" the therapist's wife asked later. "Why did you go to the child's house?"

"I don't know, except—damn it all, it wasn't anything he said, but something screamed at me that this time he meant to kill himself. He signaled me but I don't know how— maybe it was in his face or his eyes or his hands. Maybe even the way he held himself and the fact that he didn't laugh at a joke I made, a good joke. He didn't have to use words. Everything about him told me that this time he meant it."

This incident happened not today nor within the last ten years, but twenty years ago. Today almost any good therapist would not only receive the message, but also know just how the message was sent, just what clue the boy had given him.

The empty face, the listless posture, the crossed hands, would all have spelled out a meaning as clearly as any speech. In body language the boy was telling the therapist what he meant to do. Words were no longer of any use. He had used them to cry out to no avail too often and had to fall back on a more primitive, more basic way of conveying his message.

What Does Your Posture Say?

In the twenty years since this incident took place, psychologists have become increasingly aware of how useful and important body language is in therapy. Interestingly enough, while many of them use body language in their practice, few are aware of doing so and many have no idea of all the work that has been done in the field of kinesics by men like Dr. Scheflen and Dr. Ray L. Birdwhistell.

Dr. Birdwhistell, professor of research in anthropology also at Temple University, who has initiated most of the basic work in developing a notational system for the new science of kinesics, warns that "no body position or movement, in and of itself, has a precise meaning." In other words, we cannot always say that crossed arms mean, "I will not let you in," or that rubbing the nose with a finger means disapproval or rejection, that patting the hair means approval and steepling the fingers superiority. These are naïve interpretations of kinesics, and tend to make a parlor game out of a science. Sometimes they are true and sometimes they are not, but they are only true in the context of the entire behavior pattern of a person.

Body language and spoken language, Dr. Birdwhistell believes, are dependent on each other. Spoken language alone will not give us the full meaning of what a person is saying, nor for that matter will body language alone give us the full meaning. If we listen only to the words when someone is talking, we may get as much of a distortion as we would if we listened only to the body language.

Psychiatrists particularly, according to Dr. Birdwhistell, must listen to both the body language and the spoken language. In an attempt to teach them how to do this, he published a paper called "Communication Analysis in the Residency Setting," in which he explains some of the methods he has used to make residents, young learning doctors, aware of the communication potential of body language.

It is an interesting aside that Dr. Birdwhistell has helped develop the concept of a "moral looking time." He believes that one person can observe another's eyes, face, abdomen, legs and other parts of the body for only so long before tension is created in both observer and observed.

In his advice to residents he points out that almost every moving part of the body can contain some message for the doctor, but when all else fails he falls back on two classic examples of body language that can communicate.

One, he explains, is the young adolescent girl who has to learn what to do with her newly developed breasts. How should she hold them? Thrust proudly forward with her shoulders back? Or should she pull her shoulders forward and hide her breasts by flattening them out? What should she do with her arms and shoulders, and what should she do about her mother who tells her half the time, "Hold yourself straight. Be proud of your body," and the rest of the time says, "Don't go around sticking out like that! You mustn't wear such tight sweaters."

I have a young teen-age friend who is particularly uninhibited and self-assured. Catching sight of herself in a mirror while trying on a bikini, she told her mother, "Aren't they great? Never mind cremation if I die. I'm going to have them bronzed for posterity!"

Most girls in their teens haven't this kind of body pride, and the carrying of their newly developed breasts becomes a real problem. The resident doctor can be made aware that changes in a girl's posture may signal depression, excitement, courtship, anger, or even an appeal for help. Eventually, in his own practice, he will be able to recognize and interpret some of the different problems of his teen-age patients by their stance.

Another example Dr. Birdwhistell uses for residents is what he calls the "remarkable distensibility and contractibility of the male abdomen and belly."

In courtship we have seen that the male will tighten his abdominal muscles and pull in his belly. In depression he may over-relax these muscles and let his stomach hang out. The degree of tension of these muscles can tell a great deal about the emotional and mental condition of a man. We must realize that the entire body is to body language as the speech organs are to the spoken language.

Dr. Paul L. Wachtel of the Downstate Medical Center, State University of New York, has studied nonverbal communication in psychiatric patients and has published an article titled, "An Approach to the Study of Body Language in Psychotherapy."

Each movement or position of the body, according to Dr. Wachtel, has adaptive, expressive and defensive functions, some conscious and some unconscious. "We seek," he said, "a thorough clinical evaluation of the significance of the patient's use of his body."

To obtain his data Dr. Wachtel filmed psychiatric interviews and then played and replayed the films, matching body language to verbal communication. One thing he learned from watching the films was when to look for significant gestures. Theoretically you could tell by listening to a patient, but actually the movements are too fast and are often missed in an interview. Film can be slowed down and replayed, serving as a time machine to recall any part of an interview at will.

An example of how body language helps, Dr. Wachtel said, came about in an interview with an extremely troubled person who did not know how she felt about a friend with whom she was involved.

In the film he noticed that whenever she was angry she made certain gestures. When she repeated these same gestures at the mention of the friend's name he was able to show her graphically how she felt toward that friend. Understanding your emotions is, of course, the first step in handling them.

Dr. Wachtel regards body language as a conscious or unconscious attempt by the patient to communicate with the therapist. One patient he studied would lean back and clasp her hands as the therapist reached certain troublesome areas. "Perhaps," Dr. Wachtel said, "this is a relatively common expression of resistance."

Different Places, Different Postures

Accepting the idea that man uses more than one form of communication has some very definite advantages to both the psychiatrist and the ordinary citizen. The psychiatrist can learn what to expect from his patient and the ordinary citizen can learn a great deal about what to expect from his fellow men if he understands that they react on a body language level as well as on a spoken level.

This awareness of body language is often a key to personal relationships and it may be the secret so many men use in handling others. Some men seem able to interpret body language and manipulate people with their bodies as well as with their voices.

Beyond this, the awareness of someone else's body language and the ability to interpret it create an awareness of one's own body language. As we begin to receive and interpret the signals others are sending, we begin to monitor our own signals and achieve a greater control over ourselves and in turn function more effectively.

However, it is very difficult to gain control of all the different methods of communication. There are literally thousands of bits of information exchanged between human beings within moments. Our society programs us to handle these many bits of data, but on an unconscious level. If we bring them up to our consciousness we run the risk of mishandling them. If we have to think of what we are doing, it often becomes much more difficult to do it. An aware mind is not necessarily as effective as an unaware one.

In spite of this psychiatrists continue to study all aspects of body communication. Dr. Scheflen has been particularly interested in the significance of posture in communication systems. In an article in the journal *Psychiatry* he notes that the way people hold their bodies tells us a great deal about what is going on when two or more people get together.

"There are no more than about 30 traditional American gestures," Dr. Scheflen writes and adds that there are even fewer body postures which carry any significance in communication, and that each of these occurs in a limited number of situations. To make his point, he notes that a posture such as sitting back in a chair is one rarely taken by a salesman who is trying to sell something to a more influential client.

While everyone in America is familiar with all of the different postures Americans may take, this doesn't mean that everyone uses all of them. A nineteen-year-old college student from New York will use different postures than a Midwestern housewife, and a construction worker in the state of Washington will use different postures than a salesman in Chicago. Dr. Scheflen believes that a real expert in body language could tell just what part of the country a man came from by the way he moved his brow when he talked. Such an expert, however, has not yet been developed.

We are all aware of this regional difference in body language when we watch a talented mime. By specific gestures the mime can tell us not only what part of the world his character comes from, but also what he does for a living. When I was a college student in the days when football players were college heroes, many of the non-athletic boys at school would imitate the football-player walk realistically enough to arouse the girls' interest.

The Movement and the Message

Dr. Birdwhistell, in his work in kinesics, has tried to pinpoint just what gesture indicates what message. One of the things he has uncovered is that every American speaker moves his head a number of times during a conversation. If you film a typical conversation between two Americans and then slow down the film to study the elements of posture in slow motion you will notice a head movement when an answer is expected. The head movement at the end of each statement is a signal to the other speaker to start his answer.

This is one of the ways in which we guide our spoken conversations. It enables a back-and-forth exchange without the necessity of saying, "Are you finished? Now I'll talk."

Of course the signals for other regions of the world will be different. In theory it would follow that watching two people talk would give a good clue to their nationality.

In our language, a change in pitch at the end of a sentence can mean a number of things. If there is a rise in pitch, the speaker is asking a question. Ask, "What time is it?" and notice how your voice goes up on "it." "How are you?" Up on "you." "Do you like your new job?" Up on "job."

This is a linguistic marker. Dr. Birdwhistell has discovered a number of kinesic markers that supplement the linguistic markers. Watch a man's head when he asks a question. "What time is it?" His head comes up on "it." "Where are you going?" His head comes up on the "ing" in going. Like the voice, the head moves up at the end of a question.

This upward movement at the end of a question is not limited to the voice and head. The hand, too, tends to move up with the rise in pitch. The seemingly meaningless hand gestures in which we all indulge as we talk are tied in to pitch and meaning. The eyelid, too, will open wider with the last note of a question.

Just as the voice lifts up at the end of a question, it also drops in pitch at the end of a statement. "I like this book." With "book" the voice goes down. "I'd like some milk with my pie." Down on "pie."

The head also accompanies the voice down at the end of a statement, and according to Dr. Birdwhistell, so do the hand and the eyelid.

When a speaker intends to continue a statement, his voice will hold the same pitch, his head will remain straight, his eyes and hands unchanged.

These are just a few of the changes in position of the eyes, head and hands as Americans speak. Rarely, if ever, do we hold our heads in one position for longer than a sentence or two. Writers are aware of this and also aware that head movement is tied not only to what we are saying but to emotional content as well. To characterize a "cool" person, one who shows and feels no emotion, a writer will have him appear stolid, physically unmoving. James Bond, in the movies made from Ian Fleming's 007 stories, was played by Sean Connery in a motionless style. His face rarely moved, even in the face of extinction. It was an excellent characterization, since he played a man who felt no emotion.

In Jewish folklore a golem is a being who shows no expression and, of course, feels no emotion. The high-fashion model holds herself in a rigid, unnatural pose to communicate no emotional overtones. When the normal man or woman talks, however, he looks to the right, to the left, now up, now down. He blinks his eyes, lifts his eyebrows, bites his lips, touches his nose—and each movement is linked to what he is saying.

Because of the tremendous variation in individual movements it is often difficult to link a specific movement to a specific message, but it is still true enough, to paraphrase Marshall McLuhan, the movement is the message. Dr. Scheflen, in studying psychiatric therapy sessions, has found that when a therapist explains something to a patient he may use one head position, but when he interprets some remark or behavior he uses another position. When he interrupts the patient he uses still a third and he has a fourth head position for listening.

The patient, too, when listening to the therapist, takes certain definite positions. In one situation studied by Dr. Scheflen, the patient put his head to the right when he acted in a childish fashion, and he kept his head erect when he spoke aggressively and maturely.

The difficulty in studying and interpreting these movements is that they are personal kinesic motions, related to events in the background of this or that particular patient. Not all patients put their heads to one side when they act childishly, and not all therapists make the same head motion when they listen. Yet it is pretty certain that the same man will repeat the same motion over and over. Dr. Scheflen was surprised that these head movements which were repeated again and again during a thirty-minute interview were so stereotyped and rigid, yet he emphasizes that in this, as well as in many other sessions he has studied, the patient and doctor rarely used a great range of movement.

It should not then be too difficult to find specific positions for a person and then relate them to statements or types of statements, questions, answers, explanations, etc.

Postures and Presentations

Movements of the head, the eyelids and the hands are not really postural movements, and Dr. Scheflen calls them "points." A sequence of several points he labels a "position" which is much closer to a posture. A position, he says, consists of "a gross postural shift involving at least half the body." A position can last for about five minutes.

Most people in a social situation will run through two to four positions, although Dr. Scheflen has observed psychotherapists in a treatment situation hold one position for as long as twenty minutes.

To illustrate the use of positions, imagine a situation in which one man is holding forth on a particular subject. The listener leans back in his chair, arms and legs crossed, as he listens to the speaker's ideas. When the listener reaches a point where he disagrees with the speaker, he shifts his position in preparation for delivering his protest. He may lean forward and uncross his arms and legs. Perhaps he will raise one hand with the forefinger pointed as he begins to launch a rebuttal. When he is finished he will again lean back into his first position, arms and legs crossed—or perhaps into a third, more receptive position where his arms and legs are uncrossed as he leans back, signaling that he is open to suggestion.

If you take all the positions a man or a woman goes through during the course of a conversation, you have what Dr. Scheflen labels a "presentation." A presentation can last up to a few hours, and is terminated by a complete change in location. Leaving the room, going to make a phone call, to get cigarettes, to the washroom—any move to cut the conversation short ends a presentation. If the person returns, then a new presentation starts.

The function of posture in communication, Dr. Scheflen believes, is to mark these units, points, positions, and presentations. The units themselves serve as punctuation for a conversation. Different positions are related to different emotional states, and often emotional states can be recaptured when a person resumes the original position in which they occurred. The careful and observant psychotherapist will realize, after a while, what postures are associated with what emotional states. This reflects the same thing Dr. Wachtel found. The woman he studied made a definite gesture when she was angry.

The ordinary citizen who understands body language very well, and uses it, has a grasp of these postures, though he may be unaware of it, and he can relate them to the emotional states of the people he knows. In this way he can actually keep a step ahead of other people in his dealings with them. This art can be taught to people for it is a function of careful observation but it can only be learned if one is aware that it exists.

Before posture was analyzed this carefully, psychiatrists were aware of it. The therapist in the anecdote at the beginning of this chapter was aware of a postural change in his patient. He didn't consciously know that severe suicidal depression is linked to a definite posture, a lack of animation and humor, a passivity and general drooping, but unconsciously he was aware of it, aware enough to be bothered and finally to take the steps necessary to save his patient.

Just as the lowering of the head indicates the end of a statement, or the raising of the head the end of a question, so larger postural changes indicate end points in interactions, the end of a thought, the end of a statement. For example, a shift in posture so that you are no longer facing the person to whom you are talking, often means you have finished. You want to turn your attention somewhere else for a while.

We are all familiar with this in the exaggerated form it takes when a child has had enough of a parental lecture. His, "Yeah, yeah, I know!" is accompanied by an actual, physical turning away that signals, "Enough already! Let me go!"

However, Scheflen, like Birdwhistell and the other researchers, warns that we must not try to tie up specific posture changes to specific vocal statements. We should beware of deciding that one postural shift always means this, another always that. "The meaning or function of an event," he explains, "is not contained in itself, but in its relation to its context." A shift in posture means that something is happening. It does not always tell us what is happening. We must study the shift in relation to the entire incident to find that out.

These shifts also vary from culture to culture. In Latin countries the arms may play a greater part in communication. Every statement is accompanied with sweeping hand motions. In the tighter northern countries we move our hands very little when we talk.

The other night I watched the evangelist Billy Graham on television, and I realized that he has a number of rigid, body-language postural shifts. One of his favorites is the sweeping finger. His right index-finger accompanies his words, pointing upward when he promises heavenly rewards and swooping down in a giant circle when he "nails" a point. Another favorite is both hands parallel and open, in front of his chest, moving up and down with chopping motions. The size of his audience and the number of conversions for which he is responsible leave no doubt about the effectiveness of his postures, though an objective look makes it clear that these are all well-rehearsed posturings rather than unconscious postures. The point is that they do convey an emotional context to accompany his words, they do create an "aura."

The famous movie *King Kong* had some scenes in which the giant ape moved in a surprisingly lifelike fashion. Much of this was because of the understanding of body language by the moviemakers. When Kong held Fay Wray in his palm and looked at her, he cocked his head to one side in what was a touching copy of a completely human "point."

A recognition of how important body language is in projecting a human or friendly image has led men in politically high places to adopt various body language generalities in an attempt to achieve that indefinable something we call charisma.

John Kennedy had it, and no matter what he said, a few gestures, a correct posture, captivated his audience. Robert Kennedy, not at all a tall man, came on very tall through his manipulation of posture. Johnson took lessons in body language and tried unsuccessfully to change his image and Richard Nixon, too, is very conscious of the importance of body language and tries to use it consciously to manipulate his audience. This use of body language is a blessing to the actor who mimics these politicians. David Frye, the mimic, relies heavily on these postures and posturings to make his characterizations perfect.

Jockeying for Position

Posture is not only a means of punctuating a conversation, it is also a way in which people can relate to each other when they are together. Dr. Scheflen has divided all postures that people take when they are with others into three groups: 1) inclusive-non-inclusive, 2) vis-à-vis or parallel body orientation and 3) congruence-incongruence.

Inclusiveness or *non-inclusiveness* describes the way members of a group include or do not include people. They do this by placing their bodies, arms or legs in certain positions. At a cocktail party, a group of people may form a little circle that excludes all others. If three members of a group are sitting on a couch, the two at each end can "bookend," turn inward to enclose the one in the center, and exclude others. In this way they achieve inclusiveness. They may also cross their legs to lock in their central member or members.

In the previous chapter we saw how the grandmother and daughter in a therapeutic group "bookended" the mother in order to keep her away from the advances of the therapist. This is a device often used to keep non-members out of a group, or to keep members in.

The arms and legs of group members are often unconsciously used to protect the group from intrusion. If you observe groups at any function, at weddings, parties, meetings or evenings at home, you will notice the number of curious ways group members protect their group. A man at a social gathering may place his foot up on a coffee table to act as a barrier against outsiders. Sometimes sex will determine the way in which group members exclude others. Dr. Scheflen tells of a seminar at a hospital where male staff members arranged themselves between female staff members and a male visitor. It was as if they were protecting their prized possessions from outsiders, and yet there may be no sexuality involved in this device. The female staff members are just part of a group that is automatically protected by the males.

A key to group status may be found when a group is arranged in a line on a couch, along a wall, or at a conference. The most important members will tend to be at either end.

In our discussion of personal territories we explained the significance of body zones in different cultures. When American men are in a situation where their zones or territories are violated by crowding, they often react in curious ways. Two men pushed together on a crowded couch at a party may turn their bodies away from each other, and cross their legs away. Each may put the arm that is next to his neighbor up to his face to act as a further barrier.

If a man and a woman are forced to sit very close and face to face and they are not on intimate terms, they may cross their arms and legs protectively and lean away from each other. A good way to observe these and other defenses is to experimentally move in on other people's territories at parties and see the way they react, what defenses they put up.

The second category of posture involvement, Dr. Scheflen calls *vis-à-vis* or *parallel body orientation.* Quite simply, this suggests that two people can relate to each other, posturally, by either facing each other or by sitting side by side, parallel, perhaps oriented toward a third person. If three people are involved, two will always be parallel and one facing. In groups of four, two parallel couples will face each other.

If circumstances prevent people from arranging their entire bodies in these positions, they will settle for head, and arm and leg arrangements.

The face-to-face arrangement usually occurs in a teacher-student, doctor-patient, or lover-lover relationship, where feeling or information is exchanged. Parallel arrangements usually indicate activities which require only one person. Reading, listening to a story, watching television or a show can all be done by one person alone and are also done in parallel when more than one person is involved.

Face-to-face arrangements indicate a reaction between the two people involved. Side-by-side arrangements, when they are freely taken, tell us the two people are more apt to be neutral to each other, at least in this particular situation. The way in which a couple at a party or a social gathering position themselves tells us a great deal about their relationship. In a side-by-side situation intimacy can still be achieved by facing one another with the upper half of the body.

The last category, *congruence-incongruence,* covers the ability of members of a group to imitate each other. When a group is in congruence, their body positions will be copies of each other, in some cases, mirror images.

It is interesting to note that when one member of a congruent group shifts, the others will shift with him. In general, congruence of position in a group indicates that all members are in agreement. If the group has two points of view, the advocates of each viewpoint will take different positions. Each subgroup will be congruent in itself, but non-congruent to the other subgroup.

Old friends when arguing or discussing something will adopt congruent positions to show that, in spite of the discussion, they are still friends. A husband and wife who are very close will adopt congruent postures when one is under attack. In body language, the other is saying, "I support you. I'm on your side."

People who wish to show that they are a cut above the rest of a group may deliberately take a non-congruent position. In doctor-patient, parent-child, teacher-student relationships, the postures will be non-congruent, again to show status or importance. The man at a business meeting who deliberately adopts an unusual position does this in an attempt to indicate his higher status.

I know of a top editor in a publishing house who adopts a most curious position during conferences. He leans back and clasps his hands high above his head, then keeps them behind his head, his elbows extended like wings. This at once sets him apart and indicates his status. It makes him higher than the other men at the conference.

It was pointed out to me, however, that a close subordinate of this man's will often, after a stated interval, copy the editor's exact position, saying in body language, "I am on your side. I am faithful to you, my leader." He may also be saying, "I am trying to bask in your reflected importance." There is also the possibility that he is saying, "I am trying to take over from you."

The leader at any gathering, family or social, often sets the position for the group and one by one the others fall in. In a family, if the wife sets the position, then the chances are that she has the strongest hand in decision-making and, in effect, wears the pants in the family.

Three Clues to Family Behavior

Study the table arrangements of a family carefully. Who takes a seat first and where? A psychologist friend of mine who has made a study of table seating analyzed the positioning of a family of five in terms of the family relationships.

"In this family," he explained, "the father sits at the head of the table, and he is also the dominant member of the family. His wife is not in competition with him for dominance, and she sits to his immediate right. The rationale is that they are close enough to share some intimacy at the table, and yet they are also close to the children.

"Now the positioning of the children is interesting. The eldest girl who is in competition with the mother for the father's affection, on an unconscious level, sits to the father's left, in congruence with the mother's position.

"The youngest, a boy, is interested in his mother, a normal situation for a boy, and he sits to her right, a space away from his father. The middle child, a girl, sits to her sister's left. Her position at the table, like her position in the family, is ambivalent."

What is interesting about this arrangement is the unconscious placement of all the members in accordance with interfamily relationships. This selecting position can start as early as the selecting of a table. There is more jockeying for dominance possible around an oblong table than around a round one.

The positioning of the husband and wife is important in

understanding the family set-up. A husband and wife at either end of a long table are usually in conflict over the dominant position in the family, even if the conflict exists on an unconscious level.

When the husband and wife choose to sit catercornered, they are usually secure in their marital roles and have settled their conflict one way or the other. Which one sits at the head?

Of course if the table is small and they face each other across it, this may be the most comfortable position for intimacy.

Positions at a table can give a clue to dominance within a family. Another clue to interfamily relationships lies in the tightness or looseness of a family.

A photographer friend of mine was recently assigned to shoot some informal pictures of a mayoral candidate in a large Midwestern city. He spent a day with the family and came away muttering unhappily.

"Maybe I got one decent shot," he told me. "I asked him to call his dog and it was the only time he relaxed."

Asked to explain, my friend said, "The house was one of those up-tight places, the tightest one I've ever been in. Plastic covers on the lamp shades, everything in place, everything perfect—his damned wife followed me around picking up flashbulbs and catching the ashes from my cigarettes in a tray. How could I get a relaxed shot?"

I knew what he meant for I have seen many homes like that, homes that represent a "closed" family. Everything about the family is closed in, tight. Even the postures they take are rigid and unbending. Everything is in place in these neat, formal homes.

We can usually be sure that the family in such a home is

less spontaneous, more tense, less likely to have liberal opinions, to entertain unusual ideas and far more likely to conform to the standards of the community.

By contrast the "open" family will have a lived-in look to their house, an untidy, perhaps disorganized appearance. They will be less rigid, less demanding, freer and more open in thought and action.

In the closed family each member is likely to have his own chair, his own territory. In the open family it seldom matters who sits where. Whoever gets there first belongs.

On a body language level the closed family signals its tightness by its tight movements, its formal manner and careful posture. The open family signals its openness by looser movements, careless postures and informal manners. Its body language cries out, "Relax. Nothing is very important. Be at ease."

The two attitudes are reflected in a tactile sense by the mother's behavior with her children. Is she a tense, holding mother or a relaxed, careless one? Her attitude influences her children and is reflected in their behavior.

These, of course, are the two extreme ends. Most families fall somewhere in between, have some amount of openness and some closedness. Some are equally balanced and some incline toward one or the other end of the scale. The outsider studying any family can use openness or closedness as a clue to understanding it. A third and equally significant clue is family imitation.

Who imitates whom in the family? We mentioned before that if the wife sets the pace by initiating certain movements which the rest of the family follow, then she is probably the dominant partner.

Among brothers and sisters dominance can be easily

spotted by watching the child who makes the first move and noticing those who follow.

Respect in a family can be understood by watching how body language is copied. Does the son copy the father's gestures? The daughter the mother's? If so we can be reasonably sure the family set-up is in good shape. Watch out when the son begins to copy the mother's movements, the daughter her father's. These are early body language warnings. "I am off on the wrong track. I need to be set straight."

The thoughtful psychologist, treating a patient, will try to discover something of the entire family set-up and, most important, of the place of his patient in the family.

To treat a patient as an individual aside from his family is to have little understanding of the most important area of his life, his relationship to his family.

Some psychologists are beginning to insist on therapy that includes the entire family, and it is not unlikely that someday therapists will only treat patients within the framework of the family so that they can see and understand all the familial relationships and understand how they have influenced the patient.

Our first relationship is to our family, our second to the world. We cannot understand the second without thoroughly exploring the first.

9
Winking, Blinking and Nods

The Stare that Dehumanizes

The cowpuncher sat his horse loosely and his fingers hovered above his gun while his eyes, ice cold, sent chills down the rustler's back.

A familiar situation? It happens in every western novel, just as in every love story the heroine's eyes *melt* while the hero's eyes *burn* into hers. In literature, even the best literature, eyes are *steely, knowing, mocking, piercing, glowing* and so on.

Are they really? Are they ever? Is there such a thing as a burning glance, or a cold glance or a hurt glance? In truth there isn't. Far from being windows of the soul, the eyes are physiological dead ends, simply organs of sight and no more, differently colored in different people to be sure, but never really capable of expressing emotion in themselves.

And yet again and again we read and hear and even tell

of the eyes being wise, knowing, good, bad, indifferent. Why is there such confusion? Can so many people be wrong? If the eyes do not show emotion, then why the vast literature, the stories and legends about them?

Of all parts of the human body that are used to transmit information, the eyes are the most important and can transmit the most subtle nuances. Does this contradict the fact that the eyes do not show emotion? Not really. While the eyeball itself shows nothing, the emotional impact of the eyes occurs because of their use and the use of the face around them. The reason they have so confounded observers is because by length of glance, by opening of eyelids, by squinting and by a dozen little manipulations of the skin and eyes, almost any meaning can be sent out.

But the most important technique of eye management is the look, or the stare. With it we can often make or break another person. How? By giving him human or nonhuman status.

Simply, eye management in our society boils down to two facts. One, we do not stare at another human being. Two, staring is reserved for a non-person. We stare at art, at sculpture, at scenery. We go to the zoo and stare at the animals, the lions, the monkeys, the gorillas. We stare at them for as long as we please, as intimately as we please, but we do not stare at humans if we want to accord them human treatment.

We may use the same stare for the side-show freak, but we do not really consider him a human being. He is an object at which we have paid money to stare, and in the same way we may stare at an actor on a stage. The real man is masked too deeply behind his role for our stare to bother either him or us. However, the new theater that brings the actor down into the audience often gives us an uncomfortable feeling. By virtue of involving us, the audience, the actor suddenly loses his non-person status and staring at him becomes embarrassing to us.

As I said before, a Southern white may stare at a black in the same way, making him, by the stare, into an object rather than a person. If we wish pointedly to ignore someone, to treat him with an element of contempt, we can give him the same stare, the slightly unfocused look that does not really see him, the cutting stare of the socially elite.

Servants are often treated this way as are waiters, waitresses and children. However, this may be a mutually protective device. It allows the servants to function efficiently in their overlapping universe without too much interference from us, and it allows us to function comfortably without acknowledging the servant as a fellow human. The same is true of children and waiters. It would be an uncomfortable world if each time we were served by a waiter we had to introduce ourselves and indulge in social amenities.

A Time for Looking

With unfamiliar human beings, when we acknowledge their humanness, we must avoid staring at them, and yet we must also avoid ignoring them. To make them into people rather than objects, we use a deliberate and polite inattention. We look at them long enough to make it quite clear that we see them, and then we immediately look away. We are saying, in body language, "I know you are there," and a moment later we add, "But I would not dream of intruding on your privacy."

The important thing in such an exchange is that we do

not catch the eye of the one whom we are recognizing as a person. We look at him without locking glances, and then we immediately look away. Recognition is not permitted.

There are different formulas for the exchange of glances depending on where the meeting takes place. If you pass someone in the street you may eye the oncoming person till you are about eight feet apart, then you must look away as you pass. Before the eight foot distance is reached, each will signal in which direction he will pass. This is done with a brief look in that direction. Each will veer slightly, and the passing is done smoothly.

For this passing encounter Dr. Erving Goffman in *Behavior in Public Places* says that the quick look and the lowering of the eyes is body language for, "I trust you. I am not afraid of you."

To strengthen this signal, you look directly at the other's face before looking away.

Sometimes the rules are hard to follow, particularly if one of the two people wears dark glasses. It becomes impossible to discover just what they are doing. Are they looking at you too long, too intently? Are they looking at you at all? The person wearing the glasses feels protected and assumes that he can stare without being noticed in his staring. However, this is a self-deception. To the other person, dark glasses seem to indicate that the wearer is always staring at him.

We often use this look-and-away technique when we meet famous people. We want to assure them that we are respecting their privacy, that we would not dream of staring at them. The same is true of the crippled or physically handicapped. We look briefly and then look away before the stare can be said to be a stare. It is the technique we use for any unusual situation where too long a stare would be embarrassing. When we see an interracial couple we use this technique. We might use it when we see a man with an unusual beard, with extra long hair, with outlandish clothes, or a girl with a minimal mini-skirt may attract this look-and-away.

Of course the opposite is also true. If we wish to put a person down we may do so by staring longer than is acceptably polite. Instead of dropping our gazes when we lock glances, we continue to stare. The person who disapproves of interracial marriage or dating will stare rudely at the interracial couple. If he dislikes long hair, short dresses or beards he may show it with a longer-than-acceptable stare.

The Awkward Eyes

The look-and-away stare is reminiscent of the problem we face in adolescence in terms of our hands. What do we do with them? Where do we hold them? Amateur actors are also made conscious of this. They are suddenly aware of their hands as awkward appendages that must somehow be used gracefully and naturally.

In the same way, in certain circumstances, we become aware of our glances as awkward appendages. Where shall we look? What shall we do with our eyes?

Two strangers seated across from each other in a railway dining car have the option of introducing themselves and facing a meal of inconsequential and perhaps boring talk, or ignoring each other and desperately trying to avoid each other's glance. Cornelia Otis Skinner, describing such a situation in an essay, wrote, "They re-read the menu, they fool with the cutlery, they inspect their own fingernails as if seeing them for the first time. Comes the inevitable moment when glances meet, but they meet only to shoot instantly away and out the window for an intent view of the passing scene."

This same awkward eye dictates our looking behavior in elevators and crowded buses and subway trains. When we get on an elevator or train with a crowd we look briefly and then look away at once without locking glances. We say, with our look, "I see you. I do not know you, but you are a human and I will not stare at you."

In the subway or bus where long rides in very close circumstances are a necessity, we may be hard put to find some way of not staring. We sneak glances, but look away before our eyes can lock. Or we look with an unfocused glance that misses the eyes and settles on the head, the mouth, the body—for any place but the eyes is an acceptable looking spot for the unfocused glance.

If our eyes do meet we can sometimes mitigate the message with a brief smile. The smile must not be too long or too obvious. It must say, "I am sorry we have looked, but we both know it was an accident."

Bedroom Eyes

The awkward eye is a common enough occurrence for all of us to have experienced it at one time or another. Almost all actions and interactions between humans depend on mutual glances. The late Spanish philosopher José Ortega y Gasset, in his book *Man and People*, spoke of "the look" as something that comes directly from within a man "with the straight-line accuracy of a bullet." He felt that the eye, with its lids and socket, its iris and pupil, was equivalent to a "whole theatre with its stage and actors."

The eye muscles, Ortega said, are marvelously subtle and

because of this every glance is minutely differentiated from every other glance. There are so many different looks that it is nearly impossible to name them, but he cited, "the look that lasts but an instant and the insistent look; the look that slips over the surface of the thing looked at and the look that grips it like a hook; the direct look and the oblique look whose extreme form has its own name, 'looking out of the corner of one's eye.'"

He also listed the "sideways glance" which differs from any other oblique look although its axis is still on the bias.

Every look, Ortega said, tells us what goes on inside the person who gives it, and the intent to communicate with a look is more genuinely revealing when the sender of the look is unaware of just how he sends it.

Like other researchers into body language Ortega warned that a look in itself does not give the entire story, even though it has a meaning. A word in a sentence has a meaning too, but only in the context of the sentence can we learn the complete meaning of the word. So too with a look. Only in the context of an entire situation is a look entirely meaningful.

There are also looks that want to see but not be seen. These the Spanish philosopher called sideways glances. In any situation we may study someone and look as long as we wish, providing the other person is not aware that we are looking, providing our look is hidden. The moment his eyes move to lock with ours, our glance must slide away. The more skilled the person, the better he is at stealing these sideways glances.

In a charming description Ortega labels one look "the most effective, the most suggestive, the most delicious and enchanting." He called it the most complicated because it is not only furtive, but it is also the very opposite of furtive, because it makes it obvious that it is looking. This is the look given with lidded eyes, the sleepy look or calculating look or appraising look, the look a painter gives his canvas as he steps back from it, what the French call *les yeux en coulisse.*

Describing this look, Ortega said the lids are almost three-quarters closed and it appears to be hiding itself, but in fact the lids compress the look and "shoot it out like an arrow."

"It is the look of eyes that are, as it were, asleep but which behind the cloud of sweet drowsiness are utterly awake. Anyone who has such a look possesses a treasure."

Ortega said that Paris throws itself at the feet of anyone with this look. Louis XV's DuBarry was supposed to have had it, and so was Lucien Guitry. In our own Hollywood, Robert Mitchum certainly had it and it set him up for years as a masculine sex symbol. Mae West copied it and the French actress Simone Signoret has it so perfectly controlled that even in middle age she comes across as a very sexy and attractive woman.

Other Cultures, Other Looks

The recognition of the eye as a means of communication, or of a look as having special significance is nothing new. Looking is something that has always had strong emotions attached to it and has been forbidden, under certain circumstances, in prehistory and legend. Lot's wife was turned to a pillar of salt for looking back, and Orpheus lost Eurydice by looking at her. Adam, when he tasted the fruit of knowledge, was afraid to look at God.

The significance of looking is universal, but usually we are not sure of just how we look or how we are looked at. Honesty demands, in our culture, that we look someone straight in the eye. Other cultures have other rules, as a principal in a New York City high school recently discovered.

A young girl at the high school, a fifteen-year-old Puerto Rican, had been caught in the washroom with a group of girls suspected of smoking. Most of the group were known troublemakers, and while this young girl, Livia, had no record, the principal after a brief interview was convinced of her guilt and decided to suspend her with the others.

"It wasn't what she said," he reported later. "It was simply her attitude. There was something sly and suspicious about her. She just wouldn't meet my eye. She wouldn't look at me."

It was true. Livia at her interview with the principal stared down at the floor in what was a clear-cut guilty attitude and refused to meet his eyes.

"But she's a good girl," Livia's mother insisted. Not to the school, for she was too much of a "troublemaker" the principal felt, to come to the authorities with her protest. Instead, she turned to her neighbors and friends. As a result there was a demonstration of Puerto Rican parents at the school the next morning and the ugly stirrings of a threatened riot.

Fortunately, John Flores taught Spanish literature at the school, and John lived only a few doors from Livia and her family. Summoning his own courage, John asked for an interview with the principal.

"I know Livia and her parents," he told the principal. "And she's a good girl. I am sure there has been some mistake in this whole matter."

"If there was a mistake," the principal said uneasily, "I'll be glad to rectify it. There are thirty mothers outside yelling for my blood. But I questioned the child myself, and if ever I saw guilt written on a face—she wouldn't even meet my eyes!"

John drew a sigh of relief, and then very carefully, for he was too new in the school to want to tread on toes, he explained some basic facts of Puerto Rican culture to the principal.

"In Puerto Rico a nice girl, a good girl," he explained, "does not meet the eyes of an adult. Refusing to do so is a sign of respect and obedience. It would be as difficult for Livia to look you in the eye as it would be for her to misbehave, or for her mother to come to you with a complaint. In our culture, this is just not accepted behavior for a respectable family."

Fortunately the principal was a man who knew how to admit that he was wrong. He called Livia and her parents and the most vocal neighbors in and once again discussed the problem. In the light of John Flores' explanation it became obvious to him that Livia was not avoiding his eyes out of defiance, but out of a basic demureness. Her slyness, he now saw, was shyness. In fact, as the conference progressed and the parents relaxed, he realized that Livia was indeed a gentle and sweet girl.

The outcome of the entire incident was a deeper, more meaningful relationship between the school and the community—but that of course is another story. What is of particular interest in this story is the strange confusion of the principal. How did he so obviously misinterpret all the signals of Livia's behavior?

Livia was using body language to say, "I am a good girl. I

respect you and the school. I respect you too much to an-swer your questions, too much to meet your eyes with shameless boldness, too much to defend myself. But surely my very attitude tells you all this."

How could such a clear-cut message be interpreted as, "I defy you. I will not answer your questions. I will not look you in the eyes because I am a deceitful child. I will evade your questions slyly—"

The answer of course is a cultural one. Different cultures have different customs and, of course, different body lan-guage. They also have different looks and different mean-ings to the same looks.

In America, for instance, a man is not supposed to look at a woman for any length of time unless she gives him her permission with a body language signal, a smile, a backward glance, a direct meeting of his eye. In other countries differ-ent rules apply.

In America, if a woman looks at a man for too long a pe-riod of time, she commits herself to a verbal approach. Her signal says, "I am interested. You can approach me." In Latin countries, though freer body movements are permissi-ble, such a look might be a direct invitation to a physical "pass." It becomes obvious then why a girl like Livia would not look the principal in the eye.

Again, in our country, two men are not allowed to stare at each other for more than a brief period of time unless they intend to fight or to become intimate. Any man who looks at another man for too long embarrasses and annoys him and the other man begins to wonder just what he wants.

This is another example of the rigidity of the rules of looking. If someone stares at us and we meet his eye and catch him staring, it is his duty to look away first. If he does not look away as we engage his eye, then we become uncomfortable and aware that something is wrong. Again we become embarrassed and annoyed.

A Long Look at Oneself

In an attempt to discover just how some of these rules for visual communication work, Dr. Gerhard Neilson of Copenhagen analyzed the "looks" of the subjects in his self-confrontation studies. To discover just how long, and when, the people being interviewed looked at the interviewer, he filmed interviews and replayed them a number of times in slow motion.

While he started with no clear-cut idea of how long one man would look at another during an interview, he was surprised to find how little looking there actually was. The man who looked at his interviewer the most, still looked away 27 per cent of the time. The man who looked at his interviewer the least looked away 92 per cent of the time. Half of the people interviewed looked away for half of the time they were being interviewed.

Dr. Neilson found that when people spoke a lot they looked at their partners very little; when they listened a lot they also looked a lot. He reports that he expected people to look at each other more when they listened more, but he was surprised to find them looking less when they spoke more.

He found that when people start to speak, they look away from their partners at first. There is a subtle timing, he explains, in speaking, listening, looking and looking away. Most people look away either immediately before or after the beginning of one out of every four speeches they make. A few look away at the beginning of half their speeches. As they finish speaking, half the people look at their partners.

As to why so many people refuse to meet the eyes of their partners during a conversation, Dr. Neilson believes this is a way of avoiding distraction.

How Long Is a Glance?

Another study, carried out by Dr. Ralph V. Exline at the University of Delaware, involved 40 men and 40 women, all freshmen and sophomores. In the study a man interviewed 20 men and 20 women and a woman interviewed the other 20 of each sex. Half the students were questioned by both interviewers about intimate subjects, their plans, desires, needs and fears. The other half were asked about recreational interests, reading, movies, sports.

Dr. Exline found that when the students were interviewed about personal subjects, they didn't look at the interviewer as often as they did when they were interviewed about recreational subjects. Women, however, in both types of interview, looked at the interviewers more frequently than men did.

What seems to come across from both these studies, and others of a similar nature, is that when someone looks away while he's speaking, it generally means he's still explaining himself and doesn't want to be interrupted.

A locking of his gaze with his partner's at this point would be a signal to interrupt when he paused. If he pauses and is not looking at his conversational partner, it means he hasn't yet finished. He is signaling, "This is what I want to say. What is your answer?"

If you look away from the person who is speaking to you while you are listening, it is a signal, "I am not completely satisfied with what you are saying. I have some qualifications."

If you look away while you are speaking it may mean, "I am not certain of what I am saying."

If while you are listening, you look at the speaker, you signal, "I agree with you," or "I am interested in what you are saying."

If while you are speaking, you look at the listener, you may be signaling, "I am certain of what I am saying."

There are also elements of concealment in looking away from your partner. If you look away while he is speaking, you signal, "I don't want you to know what I feel." This is particularly true if the partner is critical or insulting. It is something like an ostrich burying his head in the sand. "If I cannot see you, you cannot hurt me." This is the reason children will often refuse to look at you when you are scolding them.

However, there are more complexities here than meet the eye . . . or the glance. Looking away during a conversation may be a means of concealing something. Therefore when someone else looks away, we may think he is concealing something. To practice deceit we may sometimes deliberately look at our partner instead of refusing to meet his glance.

In addition to length and direction of glances, there is a good deal of signaling involved in the act of closing the lid. In addition to the half-lidded look Ortega described, Birdwhistell states that five young nurses, in a series of tests, reported twenty-three different positions of lid closure that they could distinguish.

But they all agreed that only four out of the twenty-three "meant anything." Retesting allowed Dr. Birdwhistell to label these four positions, "open-eyed, droopy-lidded, squinting, eyes-closed-tight."

Working from the opposite end, trying to get the girls to reproduce the lid positions, was not so successful. All could reproduce five of the twenty-three positions, but only one could reproduce more than five.

Using a group of men in the same type of experiment, he found that all could reproduce at least ten positions. Unexpectedly men were more facile at winking. Some of the men could reproduce fifteen different positions, and one—fantastically eloquent in body language—came up with thirty-five different eyelid positions.

Branching out into cultural comparisons Dr. Birdwhistell found that among the Japanese both sexes were similar in the number of eyelid positions they could reproduce. But even the Japanese could recognize, in others, more positions than they could assume themselves.

When movement of the eyebrows is added to movement of the lids, many more recognizable signals are produced. Some scientists have found as many as forty different positions of the brows alone, though most agree that less than half of them are significant. It is only when the significant eyebrow movements are combined with the significant lid movements and we add forehead creases that the permutations and combinations are endless.

If each combination has a different implication, then there is no end to the number of signals we can transmit with our eyes and the skin around them.

10

An Alphabet
for Movement

Is There a Language of Legs?

As kinesics and body language became more generally known and understood, what started as a curiosity soon became a science, what started as an observable fact soon became a measurable fact, and also, unfortunately, what became a science also became an exploitable situation.

The fact that in times of stress a baby will suck his thumb, a man will bite his nails or knuckle, a woman will spread her hand across her chest are all curious gestures but an understanding of body language makes us realize that the child is sucking his thumb for security in a symbolic return to the comfort of the mother's breast. The man has substituted the socially acceptable nail-biting or knuckle-biting for the unacceptable thumb-sucking, and the woman spreads her hand across her chest in a defensive manner, covering and protecting her vulnerable breasts. An understanding of the forces behind these gestures is the point at which a curiosity becomes a science.

Knowing that people lift their eyebrows or lower their lids part way to express an emotion is an observable fact. Knowing the exact degree of lift or the angle of lowering makes the fact a measurable one. Dr. Birdwhistell has written, " 'droopy lidded' combined with 'bilaterally raised median portion depressed brows' has an evident differential meaning from 'droopy lidded' combined with a 'low unilateral brow lift.' " This is a measured explanation of the observed fact that when the eyes are half closed and both the eyebrows are raised at the ends and lowered in the centers the face looks different than it does when the eyes are half closed and one eyebrow is slightly raised.

Unfortunately, something like kinesics, related facts on the way to becoming a science, also runs the risk of being exploited. For example, just how much can we really tell from crossed legs? Earlier in the book we spoke of the use of crossed legs to unconsciously include or exclude members of a group. We have seen how they can also be used in congruent sittings where one person in a room will set a postural pattern and the others will imitate it. If the leader crosses his legs, the others will cross theirs.

Can crossed legs also express character? Do we, in the way we hold our legs when we sit, give a clue to our inner nature?

As with all body language signals, there is no simple yes-or-no answer. Crossed legs or parallel legs can be a clue to what the person is feeling, to the emotional state *at the moment,* but they may also mean nothing at all. I have a friend who is a writer and writes in longhand. He only crosses his legs from left to right, the left leg on top, never the other way. At a recent social evening my friend was sitting to the left of his wife, his left leg over his right pointing to her. Her right leg, crossed over her left knee, pointed to him.

An amateur psychologist in the group nodded at the couple and said, "See, they form a closed circle, their crossed legs pointing to each other and excluding the rest of the group—a perfect illustration of body language."

I took my writer friend aside later and said, "I know you get along well with your wife, but I wonder about this leg crossing."

Grinning, he explained. "I can only cross my left leg over my right. It's because I write my first drafts in longhand, not on a typewriter."

Puzzled, I asked, "But what does that have to do with it?"

"I can only cross from left to right because all my life I've crossed my legs that way, and my leg muscles and bones have become adapted to it. If I cross the other way I am uncomfortable. Automatically now, I cross my left leg over my right knee."

"But how does writing in longhand . . . ?"

"Simple. I don't write at a desk. I compose in an easy chair. I write on a clipboard which I balance on my knee. To bring the clipboard high enough to write, I must cross my knees. Since I am right-handed, I write toward the left side. I therefore cross my legs so my left leg will be higher, left over right. I always have, and now it's the only position I'm comfortable in. So much for your body language. By chance I sat to the left of my wife tonight. On other nights I've happened to sit on her right."

The moral here is that before making any scientific judgment, all the facts should be known. If we are to attach any significance to leg crossing, we must also be aware of the physiological condition of the body. The same is true of arm crossing. There is a terrible temptation to fix a host of meanings to the direction in which we cross our arms. It seems to have been established that crossing the arms is sometimes a defensive gesture, a signal that you don't want to accept another's point of view, or a sign that you are insecure and want to defend yourself. Now these and a few others are valid interpretations, but when we come to the direction of the cross, left over right or right over left, we are on tricky ground.

Cross your arms without thinking. Some of you will put your left arm outside, some your right arm outside and, most important of all, you will always cross your arms the same way. Crossing them the other way just "feels wrong." This is because the way in which we cross our arms, left over right or right over left, is a genetic trait, an inborn trait, in the same way that using your left or right hand to write with is genetic. Folding the hands and intertwining the fingers is also genetic. Is your right thumb or left thumb on top?

Taking these points into consideration, we may be on safe ground when we use the gesture itself as a signal, but we are on uncertain ground when we speak of direction.

Most serious studies of body language have concerned themselves with the emotions transmitted by movement, not with the innate nature of the person transmitting the message. At best, the signal sent out, the body language, has been used to make a person understand himself. When it is used to try to determine personality or character rather than behavior, it seems fraught with contradictions.

The ABC of Body Language

In an attempt to outline certain aspects of body language and unify the science, or perhaps make body language into a science, Dr. Ray Birdwhistell has written a preliminary research manual on the subject, a manual he calls *An Introduction to Kinesics*. Basically, he has attempted to put together an annotational system for kinesics or body language, to break all relevant movements down to their basics and give a symbol—much the way a choreographer breaks the dance down into basic steps and gives each a symbol.

The result is a little like Egyptian pictographs, but hopefully not as hard to read. Starting with the eyes, since they are the most common source of communication in body language, he has decided that $\bigcirc$ is the best symbol for the open eye, — for the closed eye. A wink of the right eye then becomes (— $\bigcirc$), of the left eye ($\bigcirc$ —). Open eyes are ($\bigcirc$ $\bigcirc$) and so on. Dr. Birdwhistell calls each of these movements a kine, or the smallest recordable movement.

The first premise in developing this type of notational system for body language, Dr. Birdwhistell says, is to assume that all movements of the body have meaning. None are accidental. Once this is accepted, we can proceed to a study of every movement, its significance and a means of labeling it.

I find that this basic assumption is the most difficult one to accept. Perhaps scratching the nose is an indication of disagreement, but it may also be an indication of an itchy nose. This is where the real trouble in kinesics lies, in separating the significant from the insignificant gestures, the meaningful from the purely random, or from the carefully learned.

When a woman sits with her legs slanted, parallel and slightly crossed at the ankles it may indicate an orderly mind, but it is far more likely to be an affected positioning or even charm school training. Certain charm schools believe that this is a graceful and womanly pose and suggest that women condition themselves to fall into it when they sit. It is also a pose that allows a woman with a mini skirt to sit in a comfortable but unrevealing position. It was also a pose our grandmothers considered "very ladylike."

These are some of the reasons we must approach kinesics with caution and study a motion or a gesture only in terms of the total pattern of movement, and we must understand the pattern of movement in terms of the spoken language. The two, while sometimes contradictory, are also inseparable.

To standardize body movements before making them into kinesic pictographs, we must have a zero point or a resting point. An arm movement, for example, is only significant if we know how much distance it covers. We can only know this if we set up a standard zero point.

In Dr. Birdwhistell's work, he sets a zero point for "middle-class Americans." This is the semi-relaxed state of the body, head balanced and facing forward, arms at the side and legs together. Any perceptible position is a motion away from this zero point.

It is significant that Dr. Birdwhistell limits his own work to middle-class Americans. He recognizes that even in our culture there is a surprising lack of uniformity in body movement. Working-class people will give certain interpretations to movements, and these interpretations will not apply in middle-class circles.

However, in America there is, I think, a greater ethnic difference in gesture than there is a class difference. Although he does not say so specifically, I would assume that Dr. Birdwhistell is primarily concerned with body language among middle-class white Anglo-Saxon Protestant Americans. If this is so it presents serious students of the subject with an overwhelming amount of data to learn. They must absorb not only a system of interpretation for white Anglo-Saxon Protestant Americans, but also one for Italian-Americans, Jewish Americans, American Indians, black Americans and so on. Then there would be class lines in each of these categories, and the total number of systems would become overwhelming. What must be found is one common system that will work for all cultures and all ethnic groups, and I suspect that, with some variation, Dr. Birdwhistell's system will.

Dr. Birdwhistell also points out that a body movement may mean nothing at all in one context, and yet be extremely significant in another context. For example, the frown we make by creasing the skin between our eyebrows may simply mark a point in a sentence or, in another context, it may be a sign of annoyance or, in still another context, of deep concentration. Examining the face alone won't tell us the exact meaning of the frown. We must know what the frowner is doing.

Another point Dr. Birdwhistell makes is that all of our movements, if they are significant, are learned. We pick them up as a part of our society. As an illustration of the learning power of humans he considers the most common kinesic motion, that of the eyelid. We tend to think that eyelid movements are reflex movements. We squint to guard against too much light, or we blink to keep out dust and to cleanse our eyeballs.

Contradicting this, Dr. Birdwhistell cites the numerous

cases of learned eyelid movement. Fakirs in Indian religious cults can learn to look at the sun without blinking or face a dust storm without closing their lids. Girls in our society learn to "bat their eyelashes" in flirting, even when there is no need to clean the eyeball. He suggests that examples like these prove that not all lid movement is instinctive and, he adds, that lid behavior varies from culture to culture, the same as language.

An interesting fact here is that when a bilingual person changes his language, he also changes his body language, his gestures and lid movements.

Labeling the Kines

Even if, as we showed in an earlier chapter, some gestures are genetic and not learned—smiles, for example—Dr. Birdwhistell stresses that among men communication *is* a learned art, and since kinesics is concerned with those body movements that communicate, we can assume that most of kinesics is learned too.

In spite of the fact that most of Dr. Birdwhistell's analyses of body motion have come from the study of films played over and over till all casual traits are recognized and labeled, he warns against putting too much reliance on this method. If we must film motion and slow it down and replay it again and again to analyze it before we can notice certain movements—how much value is there to the motion we discover? A motion can only be meaningful if it is easily signaled and easily received. He believes that the small gestures picked up by film and missed by the human eye cannot be of much significance in communication.

There is, however, a possible subliminal value to these

gestures. We have found that often images sent too rapidly to be perceived by the conscious eye are still recognized and absorbed by the unconscious eye. This is the whole point behind the field of subliminal communication.

Dr. Birdwhistell not only makes a distinction between those gestures we notice and those we don't, but also between those we are aware of making and those we make unconsciously. There are so many possible motions we can and do make from minute to minute, that almost no one is aware of either making them or observing them. Still we send out these continual signals and we receive them and, in relation to our reception, we send out more.

The most important thing to realize about body language, according to Dr. Birdwhistell, is that no single motion ever stands alone. It is always part of a pattern. A novelist may write, "She winked at him." But the statement only has meaning because the reader is aware of all the other gestures that go with a wink, and knows, in the context of the written situation, that that particular wink means an invitation to a flirtation.

The wink alone is called by Dr. Birdwhistell a kine, the smallest measurement of body language. This particular kine can be described as "a lowering of one lid while holding the other relatively immobile." This type of description, incidentally, tends to drain the kine of all attached emotion. It becomes a simple closing of one eye instead of a signal to flirtation.

In developing a system of "writing" body language, it is necessary to drain all emotion from the movement noted. It is also necessary to work out an experimental system for recording and duplicating kines. For this Dr. Birdwhistell uses an actor or a student skilled in body language to try to project different motions and their significance to a group of students. The group is asked to differentiate between the motions, but not to guess what each motion means.

"Does this mean something different from this?" is the usual question. In this way the recorder discovers when a small range of motion projects a different impression. To that extra motion he can then assign a meaning.

From a large series of such experiments Dr. Birdwhistell has managed to separate different kines, to tell at what point an additional kine makes the whole movement different.

For example, an actor was told to face the group of students and give the following expression.

Translated into descriptive terms, this expression would be a wink with the left eye closed and a squint at the corner of the left eye. The mouth is normal, but the tip of the nose is depressed. A second, similar expression is then tried on the group of observers. Diagrammed, it would go like this:

Described: it is a wink with the right eye, a squint at the corner of the left eye, the mouth held normal and the nose depressed.

The observers were asked the difference, and their comment was, "They look different, but they don't mean anything different."

A pertinent piece of information is then added to the growing body of data about kinesics. *It doesn't matter which eye is winked. The meaning is the same. Nor does it matter if one side of the eye is squinted.*

A third instruction is then tried out on the observers.

Essentially, this is the first wink without the squint and with the tip of the nose depressed. The group of observers decided that this was the same as the first expression. The science of kinesics now understands that a squint doesn't usually mean anything in body language. Finally, a fourth variation is tried.

In this expression the wink is the same and the squint is kept at the closed eye. The tip of the nose is depressed, but the mouth is changed. It is drawn down into a pout. When this expression is shown to the group, their comment is, "Well, that changes things."

The datum that then goes into the kinesic file is, *a change in mouth position causes a change in meaning*.

Here a careful scientific study confirms the fact that communication is less likely to come from any change in the eye itself, than it is from a change in the face. We would think that squinting and alternate winking would convey different meanings, but Dr. Birdwhistell shows that they don't. A real change in expression is only reached when the mouth changes.

Of course he did not evaluate eyebrow change in this sequence. If he had, a slight change in either eyebrow might have signaled a very different meaning. A lift to one eye-

brow is a classic signal of doubt, a lift to both eyebrows, of
surprise and a lowering of both, uneasiness or suspicion.

The doctor found that winking, or closing one eye was
significant in conveying an emotion. Squinting was not significant when the mouth was held in a normal position. A
squint with a pout, however, was significant. A depressed
nose tip was not significant in the context of winked eyes,
but in other contexts it was meaningful.

Culture and Kinesics

The face, we can see, has a tremendous possible variety of
expressions, and when we draw back a bit to consider the
head, over and beyond the face, another set of motions become possible. One nods, shakes, pivots, bounces; and all
are meaningful. But all hold different meanings when combined with different facial expressions and in different cultural situations.

A friend of mine teaches in a large graduate school which
has many students from India. These students, he tells me,
move their heads up and down to signify no, and from side
to side to signify yes. "I'm sometimes driven to distraction,"
he complained, "when I explain a particularly complicated
point and they sit there signaling what I understand to be
'no' as they accept it, and what I understand to be 'yes'
when they don't accept it. Yet I know it's only a cultural
problem. They are really signaling the opposite of what I receive, but that doesn't make it any easier for me. I'm so culturally indoctrinated myself that I just cannot accept the
contradiction."

Cultural indoctrination in terms of body language is very
difficult to overcome. I know a professor of mathematics at

a nearby university who was originally a Talmudic student in Germany and left in the early 30's. To this day, when he lectures he falls back into the culture-oriented "davening" posture of the Talmudic student. He leans forward, bending his body from the waist, then rises on his toes and straightens up, arching his body backwards.

Even when this was pointed out to him in a joking manner, the professor was unable to control his body movement. We cannot underestimate the strength of cultural ties in body language. In Germany, during the Nazi years, Jews who were trying to pass as non-Jews often gave themselves away by their body language. Their hand movements were freer and more open than the Germans' hand movements, and of all the elements of their disguise, these hand movements were the hardest to control.

Because of this cultural difference, an observer of one nationality may see things in body language that are completely missed by someone of a different nationality.

The above description, open eyes with a medial brow contraction, pinched nostrils and a mouth in repose, would be the same to an American as the one below.

However, to someone from Italy, there would be a subtle difference in omitting the medial brow contraction. The first expression might suggest uneasiness or apprehension. The final clue in each case would have to come from the context in which the expression occurred.

It is always, Dr. Birdwhistell emphasizes, a case of one complementing the other, body language in the context of the spoken language giving the clue to action and understanding. And yet, no matter what the spoken language, body language can often give a clue to the dynamics of the true situation.

Follow the Leader

Dr. Birdwhistell cites the case of a gang of adolescent boys. Three boys in the gang were what the doctor called "heavy vocalizers," what we might call "loud mouths." Filming the action of this group, he found that within the gang the three "loud mouths" were responsible for from 72 to 93 per cent of all the words spoken.

There were two leaders in the gang. One of them belonged to the "loud mouths." Let's call him Tom. The other leader was a quiet fellow, Bob. In fact he was one of the quietest boys in the group. Careful analysis showed that Bob was responsible for only about 16 per cent of the words spoken. What then made him a leader?

In answering this question, we might also help to answer the more general question, what makes leadership? Is it the ability to give orders and talk others down? If that is so, as we might suspect from Tom's leadership, what about Bob who spoke so little and yet was a leader too?

The answer, Dr. Birdwhistell suspected, might lie in body language. Bob's leadership, he decided, seemed to be a kinesic one.

Studying the filmed records of the gang in action it was found that Bob, compared to the other boys, "engaged in few unrelated acts." Unrelated acts, Dr. Birdwhistell explains, are acts that try to start something new, that is, unrelated to what's being done. "Let's go fishing," when the gang is headed for a baseball game; or "Let's go downtown to the drugstore and hang around," when the gang is headed for a nearby beach.

Bob rarely took the chance of asking the gang to do something it wasn't ready to do or inclined to do. He would steer the gang in a direction it wanted to go, instead of trying to force it in a completely new direction. "Come on, let's go for a swim," if they were all sitting around on the beach, or "Let's go down to the drugstore," when they were headed for town.

There's a good lesson here in leadership. The most successful leader, in gangs or in politics, is always the one who anticipates the desired action and leads people toward it, who makes people do what they want to do. Bob was an old hand at this.

But more interesting from a body language point of view, Bob was "kinesically mature." He had less wasteful body motions than the other boys. He didn't shuffle his feet needlessly. He didn't put his hand to his mouth, scratch his head or tap his fingers. The difference between maturity and immaturity is often telegraphed by body language. Too much body movement without real meaning is immature. A mature person moves when he has to, and moves purposefully.

The type of boy who is a born leader, who leads a gang in the direction it wants to go, is also mature enough to channel his body movements into useful areas. Listening is one of these areas. Kinesically, Bob was a good listener. He would copy the posture of the boy who was talking. He would steer the conversation along with the proper facial and head movements, and he wouldn't jiggle his leg or his foot or indulge in all the youthful body language signals which mean, "I am restless, bored, disinterested."

Because of his listening ability in a body language sense, the rest of the gang were apt to go to Bob with their problems and to trust him when he made a suggestion. Oddly enough, or perhaps obviously enough, Bob, though he spoke less than the others, was a good conversationalist. It is possible that the traits of body language that made him a leader were reflected in his speech. When he did talk what he said was effective.

With this in mind, Dr. Birdwhistell has divided the body into eight sections to make these "little movements" easier to investigate. In addition to the *head*, and to the *face* with its pictographic symbols, he has the *trunk and shoulders*, the *arm and wrist* area, the *hands and fingers*, the *hip*, *leg and ankle* area, the *foot* and the *neck*.

The special signs for movement in each of these parts are combined with a number of directional signals. These include ↑ to a higher position, ↓ to a lower position, ⟶ forward, ⟵ backward and ⊣ which signals continuity of any motion or position.

But when all is said and done, the question inevitably arises: just how much does a system of notation contribute to the study of body language? How important is it to record an incident in kinesic terms? Even when the notation is combined with a record of the spoken words, there is surely only a limited use for the combination and that use is probably limited to only a few scholars.

However, such a notational system need not be confined to recording situations for study. It could, like the notational system for the dance, be used to "score" speeches and generate maximum effectiveness in fields such as politics or teaching. It could be used by therapists to "score" therapy sessions and refer back to what the patient said with his body as well as with his mouth. It could be used by actors and entertainers and even by businessmen.

In fact, when you begin to think about it, there are very few situations where such a notational system would not come in handy. Whether Dr. Birdwhistell's system will catch on or not remains to be seen, but eventually some such system will be needed.

11
Body Language: Use and Abuse

Let's Talk to the Animals

A sign of the antiquity of body language and its supremacy over the spoken word has come from the studies of a husband and wife team of researchers, R. Allen and Beatrice T. Gardner of the University of Nevada. Pondering the many failures of psychologists to teach the anthropoid apes to speak, the Gardners decided to try gestures instead. Body language is a natural part of all animal behavior, they reasoned, and apes are familiar enough with body language to learn to use gestures for communication. This is particularly true of anthropoid apes, because they are imitative and manually dextrous.

The Gardners decided to teach a young female chimpanzee named Washoe the sign language used by the deaf in North America. The chimp was given the freedom of the Gardner house along with toys and large doses of tender loving care, and she was surrounded by humans who used only sign language to communicate.

Washoe, in true chimp fashion, very quickly imitated her human friends' sign language gestures, but it took months of patient work before she could reproduce them on command. She was urged to "speak up" by touching her hand, and any "faulty diction" was improved by repeating the sign in an exaggerated way. When Washoe learned a sign correctly she was rewarded with tickling. If she was forced to work too hard, she would rebel by running way or throwing a tantrum or by biting her teacher's hand.

After two years of patient work, Washoe learned about thirty signs. She was judged to have learned a sign if she used it of her own accord in a proper fashion at least once each day for fifteen days. Washoe learned to bring her fingertips over her head to signal "more," to shake her open hand at the wrist for "hurry" and to draw her palm across her chest for "please."

She also learned the signs for hat, shoes, pants and other articles of clothing and the signs for baby, dog and cat. Surprisingly enough, she used these latter signs for new babies, dogs or cats when she met them. Once she even used the sign for dog when she heard a bark. She has also invented some simple sentences: "Go sweet" when she wants to be carried to a raspberry bush, and "Open food drink" when she wants something from the refrigerator.

The experiment is still continuing, and Washoe is learning new gestures and putting them into new sentences. The old Dr. Dolittle idea of talking to the animals may yet be possible with body language.

However, some blasé naturalists point out that body language among animals is no new thing. Birds signal sexual willingness by elaborate courtship dances, bees signal the direction of a honey supply by involved flight patterns and dogs will indulge in a host of signals from rolling over and playing dead to sitting up and begging for food.

What is new in the case of Washoe is the teaching of a language to an animal, and the animal's initiation of signs in that language. It is logical that the deaf sign language should have succeeded where a spoken language failed. Loss of hearing and the cutting off of the world of sound apparently make an individual much more sensitive to the world of gestures and motions. If this is so, then someone who is deaf should have a more sensitive understanding of body language.

Symbols in a World Without Sound

With this in mind, Dr. Norman Kagan of Michigan State University conducted a study among deaf people. They were shown films of men and women in various situations and asked to guess at the emotional state of these people and describe what body language clues they used to convey this state. Because of technical difficulties they were unable to use lip reading.

"It became apparent to us," Dr. Kagan said, "that many parts of the body, perhaps every part to some extent, reflect a person's feeling-state."

As an example, talking while moving the hands or playing with a finger ring and moving restlessly were all interpreted by the deaf as nervousness, embarrassment and anxiety. When the eyes and face suddenly "came down," when the person seemed to "swallow back" his expression, or when his features "collapsed" it was interpreted as guilt.

Excessively jerky movements were labeled frustration, and a shrinking body movement, as if "hiding oneself," spelled out depression. Forcefulness was seen as the snapping forward of the head and whole body including the arms and shoulders, and boredom was inferred when the head was tilted or rested at an angle and the fingers doodled. Reflectiveness was linked to intensity of gaze, a wrinkled forehead and a downcast look. Not wanting to see or to be seen was signaled by taking off eyeglasses or looking away.

These interpretations were given by deaf people, and sound played no part in transmitting clues, yet the interpretations were accurate. The gestures were interpreted within the total context of a scene, but the scene was played without any words. Body language alone, it seems, can serve as a means of communication if we have the ability to understand it, if we are extremely sensitive to all the different movements and signals. But this requires the supersensitivity of a deaf person. His sense of vision has become so heightened, his search for supernumerary clues so intense, that the total context of a scene can be transmitted to a deaf person through body language alone.

The real value of body language, however, still remains in a blending of all levels of communication of the spoken language, and whatever else is transmitted on the vocal wavelength, with the visual language including body language and self-imagery, with communication along any other bands. One of these other bands is the tactile, which sometimes overlaps the visual but is really a more primitive and basic form of communication.

According to the late Dr. Lawrence K. Frank of Harvard, a child's knowledge of his world starts with the touch of his mother, with caressing and kissing, the oral touch of her nipple, the warmth and security of her arms. His education proceeds with a "don't touch" indoctrination to fit him into the "property rights" aspect of his culture, to teach him a sense of possession and belonging. As a child and as an adolescent his touching of his own body, his adventures with masturbation—the ultimate self-touch—his exploration in young manhood of the touching of love, the mutual body exploration with his love partner, are all aspects of tactile communication.

But these are obvious aspects. We also communicate with ourselves tactually by scratching, patting or pressing against objects. We say, "I am aware of myself. I am giving myself pleasure and satisfaction." We communicate with others by hand-holding, handshaking and all kinds of touching, saying, "Be reassured. Be comforted. You are not alone. I love you."

Just where body language leaves off and tactile communication takes over is difficult to pinpoint. The barriers are too hazy and uncertain.

Mental Healing Through Body Language

Perhaps the greatest value of an understanding of body language lies in the field of psychiatry. Dr. Scheflen's work has shown us how important it is for therapists to use body language consciously, and Dr. Buchheimer and others have carried an understanding of body language into the areas of self-confrontation.

Dr. Buchheimer tells of a group of adult patients who were given finger paint to use as a therapeutic device. "The feel of the paint as they smeared it over the paper would free them, we hoped, from some of the inhibitions that slowed up the therapeutic process. To help them understand what was happening, we filmed them at work and then showed them the films."

One woman patient, he said, had had a bad first marriage, destroyed in part by her inability to enjoy sex. Now in her second marriage she felt that her sexual life was much better, but her marriage was still "coming apart at the seams."

Producing a violent scarlet and purple smear with her finger paints, she suddenly cried out, "How sexy that looks!" and at the same moment she crossed her legs.

When the film was played back to her and she was confronted with her own reaction to the tactile concept of sexuality, she couldn't believe that she had reacted that way. But in a discussion of the significance of leg crossing in terms of body language she agreed that this was one way of shutting out and refusing sex symbolically. This was particularly true in the context of her other actions, her comment on the "sexy" picture. She admitted that she herself still had sexual conflicts. She began to understand, from that time on, that her second marriage was suffering from the same problems as her first, and understanding this she was able to take the proper steps toward solving her problem.

Here is a classic example of how the understanding of her own use of a body language symbolic gesture opened a woman's eyes to the extent of her problems. Dr. Fritz Perls, the psychologist who originated Gestalt therapy (the psychiatric therapy that uses body language as one of its basic tools), says of his technique, "We try to get hold of the obvious, of the surface of the situations in which we find ourselves."

The basic technique of Gestalt therapy, according to Dr.

Perls, is not to explain things to the patient, but to provide him with the opportunity to understand and discover himself. To do this, Dr. Perls says, "I disregard most of the content of what the patient says and concentrate mostly on the nonverbal level, as this is the only one which is less subject to self deception." The nonverbal level, of course, is the level of body language.

As an example of what Dr. Perls means, let's eavesdrop on one of his sessions with a thirty-year-old woman. These conversations were taken from a psychiatric training film.

PATIENT: Right now I'm scared.

DOCTOR: You say you're scared, but you're smiling. I don't understand how one can be scared and smiling at the same time.

Confused, the patient's smile becomes tremulous and fades.

PATIENT: I'm also suspicious of you. I think you understand very well. I think you know that when I get scared I laugh or I kid to cover up.

DOCTOR: Well, do you have stage fright?

PATIENT: I don't know. I'm mostly aware of you. I'm afraid that—that you're going to make such a direct attack that I'm afraid you're going to get me in a corner and I'm afraid of that. I want you to be on my side.

As she says this the patient unconsciously hits her chest.

DOCTOR: You said I'd get you in a corner and you hit yourself on the chest.

Dr. Perls repeats her gesture of hitting and she stares at her hand as if seeing it for the first time, then repeats the gesture thoughtfully.

PATIENT: Uhuh.

DOCTOR: What would you like to do? Can you describe this corner you'd like to go to?

Turning to stare at the room's corners the patient is suddenly aware of it as a place she might be in.

PATIENT: Yeah, It's back in the corner, where you're completely protected.

DOCTOR: Then you would be safer there from me?

PATIENT: Well, I know that I wouldn't really. A little safer, maybe.

Still staring at the corner she nods.

DOCTOR: If you could make believe that you were in this corner, what would you do there?

For a moment she considers. A chance phrase, in a corner, has now become a physical situation.

PATIENT: I'd just sit.

DOCTOR: You'd just sit?

PATIENT: Yeah.

DOCTOR: How long would you sit?

Almost as if she were in an actual corner, the patient's position becomes that of a little girl on a stool.

PATIENT: I don't know, but it's funny that you're saying this. This reminds me of when I was a little girl. Every time I was afraid I'd feel better sitting in a corner.

DOCTOR: Okay, are you a little girl?

Again confused that her remark has been made graphic.

PATIENT: Well, no, but it's the same feeling.

DOCTOR: Are you a little girl?

PATIENT: This feeling reminds me of it.

Forcing her to face the feeling of being a little girl, the doctor continues.

DOCTOR: *Are* you a little girl?

PATIENT: No, no, no!

DOCTOR: No. How old are you?

PATIENT: Thirty.

DOCTOR: Then you're not a little girl.

PATIENT: No!

In a later scene, the doctor says:

DOCTOR: If you play dumb and stupid you force me to become more explicit.

PATIENT: That's been said to me before, but I don't buy it.

DOCTOR: What are you doing with your feet now?

PATIENT: Wiggling.

She laughs because the wiggling motion of her feet makes her realize she is pretending. The doctor laughs too.

DOCTOR: You joke now.

Later on the patient says:

PATIENT: You're treating me like I'm stronger than I am. I want you to protect me more, to be nicer to me.

Her voice is angry, but even as she says it she smiles. The doctor imitates her smile.

DOCTOR: Are you aware of your smile? You don't believe a word you're saying.

He smiles too, disarmingly, but she shakes her head.

PATIENT: Yes, I do.

She tries to keep from smiling, but the doctor has made her recognize the fact of her smile.

PATIENT: I know you don't think I'm——

DOCTOR: Sure. You're bluffing. You're a phony.

PATIENT: Do you believe—do you mean that seriously?

Now her smile is uncertain, fading.

DOCTOR: Yeah. You laugh and giggle and squirm. It's phony.

He mimics her motions, making her see them reflected in him.

DOCTOR: You put on a performance for me.

PATIENT: Oh, I resent that very much.

The smiles and giggles are gone and she is angry in voice and body.

DOCTOR: Can you express it?

PATIENT: Yes. I most certainly am not being phony. I'll admit it's hard for me to show my embarrassment. I hate being embarrassed, but I resent you calling me a phony. Just because I smile when I'm embarrassed or put in a corner doesn't mean I'm being phony.

DOCTOR: You've been yourself for the last minute.

PATIENT: Well, I'm mad at you.

She smiles again.

DOCTOR: Now that! That!

He imitates her smile.

DOCTOR: Did you do that to cover up your anger with yourself? At that minute, at that moment, you had what emotion?

PATIENT: Well, at that minute I was mad, though I wasn't embarrassed.

The important thing about this particular session is the way in which Dr. Perls picks up body language on the part of the patient, her smile, her wiggling, even her desire to sit in a corner, and holds them up to her, forcing her to face the symbolism of her own body language. He shows her that her smile and laughter are only a defense to soften her real feelings, the anger she doesn't permit herself to feel because it might be too destructive. Only at the end does she get sufficiently mad to drop her defensive smile and really express herself. This is self-confrontation in action.

What body language combined with self-confrontation can do, as these incidents show, is to make a person aware of what he is doing with his body that contradicts what he is saying with his mouth. If you are aware of what you are doing with your body, your understanding of yourself becomes much deeper and more significant. On the other hand, if you can control your body language you can cut through many of the defensive barriers with which you surround yourself.

Faking Body Language

Recently I watched a very beautiful teen-age girl at a dance and saw her stand near the wall with a girl friend, haughty, aloof and unapproachable, for all the world like the snow maiden in the fairy tale.

I knew the girl, and I knew that she was anything but cold and aloof. I asked her later why she had been so distant.

"I was distant?" she said in genuine amazement. "What about the boys? Not one of them came up and talked to me. I was dying to dance but no one asked me." A bit tragically she added, "I'm the only teen-age old maid in school. Look at Ruth. She's my age and she danced every dance, and you know her. She's a mess."

Ruth is a mess. Fat and unattractive, but ah, the secret! Ruth smiles at every boy. Ruth cuts through all shields and all defenses. Ruth makes a boy feel comfortable and assured. He knows if he asks her to dance she'll say yes. Her body language guarantees it. My beautiful young friend, so icy calm on the surface, hides the wistful shyness she feels. She signals, "Stay away. I am unapproachable. Ask me to dance at your own risk." What teen-age boy will take a chance at such a rejection? They obey the signals and turn to Ruth.

With practice my young friend may learn to smile and soften her beauty and make it attainable. She'll learn the body language to signal boys, "I can be asked, and I'll say yes." But first she must understand the signals. She must see herself as she appears to others, she must confront herself and only then can she change.

All of us can learn that if we express the *we* that we want to be, the *we* that we are hiding, then we can make ourselves more available and free ourselves.

There are many ways of doing this, ways of "faking" body language to achieve an end. All the books on self-improvement, on how to make friends, on how to make people like you, are aware of the importance of body language and the importance of faking it properly to signal, "I am a great guy. I am cool. I want to be your friend. Trust me." Learn and apply the proper signals for these messages and you guarantee social success.

The charm schools are aware of this and use the same technique to teach girls how to sit and walk and stand gracefully. If you doubt it watch a Miss America contest and see how the girls have been trained to use body language to seem charming and attractive. Sometimes it comes across as garish, but you must give them an A for trying. Their gestures are tested and accurate. They know how much can be signaled by body language.

Politicians have learned just how important body language is, and they use it to emphasize and dramatize their speeches and also to achieve a more pleasant and more acceptable personality or image. Franklin D. Roosevelt and Fiorello LaGuardia both had instinctive command of it. In spite of the fact that Roosevelt was handicapped and never allowed his body to appear in a handicapped position (well aware of the body language impact of such an appearance), he was able to use body language to transmit a controlled and self-assured image. LaGuardia transmitted another image, homey and down-to-earth, a son of the people, and all through gestures and body movement, through a startling knowledge of the vocabulary of body language, not only in English but also in Italian and Yiddish.

Some men cannot master the grammar of body language no matter how they try. Lyndon Johnson never quite got the hang of it. His arm motions were always too studied, too mannered, too much as if he were running through a memorized program.

The exaggerated use of a limited amount of body language makes Richard Nixon fair game to mimics, such as David Frye, who only need to pick up one or two of his gestures and heighten them to convey a startling imitation.

Dr. Birdwhistell, in his contribution to the book *Explorations in Communication*, states that a well-trained "linguistic-kinesiologist" should be able to tell what movements a man is making simply by listening to his voice.

If this is true then there is a rigid link between words and movements. When an orator points in a certain way he should make a corresponding statement. When, for example, Billy Graham thunders, "You will risk heaven . . . ," he points upward with one finger; and when he adds, "You will go straight to hell!" the finger descends just as we know we shall.

This is a very obvious and crude signal-to-word linkage, but nevertheless it is a proper one and the audience accepts it and is moved by it.

Just because there are proper linkages it stands to reason that some men will distort these linkages and use them inconsistently. Some men do this with words. They stutter or stammer or pitch their sound too high or too low and take all the strength out of what they say. It is just as easy to stutter or stammer kinesically and use the wrong gesture for the wrong word.

The audience may hear your words and understand them, but a good percentage of the message will be missing or distorted and you will be facing a "cold" audience. There will be no emotion in your speech, no empathy or none of that vague word, "charisma."

Just how confusing the wrong body language can be was made very clear a few years ago by the comedian Pat Paulson. Pretending to be a candidate for political office he did some delightful spoofing of the then-current candidates by flattening his voice to strip it of all emotion, deadpanning his face to further eliminate emotion and then, very cleverly, feeding the wrong body movements into his performance. The total result was a pseudopolitical disaster.

Unfortunately the same disaster can take over in earnest when a politician is either too inhibited and awkward to use the correct gestures, or just does not know them. William J. Fulbright and Arthur Goldberg have both made searching and important political contributions, but their deliveries are so lacking in the basics of proper body language that they come across as flat and uninspired. The same is true of George McGovern and to a lesser degree of Eugene McCarthy.

McCarthy's popularity is greatest among the young people who are able to cut through the way he says things to what he says. But for the bulk of the American people it is the unfortunate truth that often the way things are said, the body language used, is more important than what is being said.

The other McCarthy, Joseph McCarthy, a few decades back, had a frighteningly effective delivery, and the same grasp of the fundamentals of body language that many fundamentalist evangelists have.

George Wallace, though his politics were hard for many people to swallow, used body language during the Presidential campaign to project an "honest" image. A careful analysis of him in action, especially with the sound turned off, makes it clear that his body language shouted down the contents of his speeches.

New York's William Buckley is a man whose political philosophy is far to the right of center, but he has always had a large audience for his television appearances, an audience that is only partly right of center. His appeal is in his delivery rather than in what he delivers. In addition to the more obvious body language of hands and posture that serves politicians who must be viewed from a distance, Buckley has an excellent command of the subtler nuances of kinesics. He uses his face with remarkable facility, lifts his eyebrows, shields his eyes, twists his lips and cheeks and presents a constant variety of expressions.

The total effect is one of liveliness and animation, and adds sincerity to his statements.

John Lindsay projects the same sincerity, but his kinesic movements are turned off a bit, toned down, less exaggerated than Buckley's and with the sincerity we get a sense of calm and reassurance and something more—an engaging ingenuousness that comes from the very toning down of kinesic motion.

Ted Kennedy has the same kinesic facility, helped out as in Lindsay's and Buckley's cases with good looks. It enables him to project a boyish sincerity that may be completely at odds with what he's doing, but still melts our defenses.

Pierre Trudeau of Canada has the same sincerity, but a

greater degree of animation—probably a reflection of his French ancestry—allowing him to add another dimension to his political image. This is the sophisticate, the man-about-town, even the playboy, but all in a good sense. His body language tells us, "Look, I'm enjoying all the things you would like to enjoy. Share them vicariously."

Once you begin to look for the styles in the man, the gestures and motions and facial twists, you begin to understand just how heavily all political figures rely on body language to make their words and images acceptable. The really good ones, good in the sense that they can project any emotion with their bodies, never had to bother about what they said. It was always the way they said it that mattered.

They were all good actors, and good actors must all be experts in the use of body language. A process of elimination guarantees that only those with an excellent command of the grammar and vocabulary get to be successful.

Of course there have been notorious exceptions. Nelson Eddy was one. He became an actor in the 30's because of his singing ability, and as is the case with many singers, he never learned the basics of body language. Some of his performances (still visible on the late late late shows) show the wooden quality of his gestures, the robotlike sawing of his arms. Contrast him with Gary Cooper. Cooper also had a wooden quality, but he used it to project solidity and masculine dependability through an unconscious grasp of the proper body language movements.

Putting It All Together

As the facts about body language are studied and analyzed and it is gradually elevated to a science, it becomes available as a tool in the study of other sciences. There was a recent report, from the Fifty-fifth Annual Convention of the Speech Association of America, by Professor Stanley E. Jones in which he applied body language principles to challenge Dr. Hall's statement that a basic difference between cultures lies in the way they handle space. Latin Americans, he said, stand closer when they talk than Chinese or Negroes, and Arabs stand even closer than Latins do.

Professor Jones, after working for two years in Harlem, Chinatown, Little Italy and Spanish Harlem, all ethnic areas of Manhattan in New York City, produced evidence that this pattern changes. He believes that conditions of poverty have forced these people to change some of their cultural behavior. According to him, there is a culture of poverty that is stronger than any ethnic subcultural background.

Professor Jones, discussing his paper in a press interview, said, "When I began studying the behavior patterns for subcultures living in New York's so-called melting pot, I expected to find that they would maintain their differences. Instead I was tremendously surprised to discover that poverty conditioned them to behave with remarkable similarity."

In overcrowded areas with poor housing, Professor Jones found that virtually everybody, regardless of their ethnic background, stood about one foot apart.

Here is a sociological use of the growing science of body language in an attempt to discover how poverty affects culture. What Professor Jones's findings seem to indicate is that the culture of the American poor overrides ethnic and national distinctions. America has become a melting pot, but it is the quality of poverty that melts down the barriers to produce a common body language.

It would be interesting to take this work further and see what other areas besides space are influenced by poverty, or to carry it in the other direction and see if wealth also breaks down the ethnic rules of body language. Are the forces of economics stronger than those of culture?

There are any number of possible studies open to the future student of body language, and the beauty of it all is that a minimal amount of equipment is necessary. While I know of a number of sophisticated studies that have been done with videotape and sixteen millimeter film and dozens of student volunteers, I also know of a perfectly charming project done by a fourteen-year-old boy whose bedroom overlooked a street telephone booth in New York City.

He used an eight millimeter motion picture camera to film as much footage of people using the booth as his allowance would permit, and he then used the family projector to slow up motion while he noted and identified each movement.

I know another, older student who is working toward his doctorate by studying the way people avoid each other on a crowded street and on a not-so-crowded street.

"When there is enough space," he explained, "they wait till they're about ten feet apart and then each gives the other a signal so they can move around each other in opposite directions." He hasn't yet discovered the exact signal or how it is used to convey which direction each will take.

Sometimes of course the signals are confused and the two people come face to face and both move to the right and then to the left in unison and keep up this silly dance till they stop, smile apologetically and then move on. Freud called it a sexual encounter. My friend calls it kinesic stuttering.

Body language as a science is in its infancy, but this book has explored some of the ground rules. Now that you know them, take a close look at yourself and your friends and family. Why do you move the way you do? What does it signify? Are you dominant or subservient in your kinesic relationship to others? How do you manage space? Are you its master or do you let it control you?

How do you manage space in a business situation? Do you knock on your boss's door and then walk in? Do you come up to his desk and dominate him, or do you stop at a respectful distance and let him dominate you? Do you allow him to dominate you as a means of placating him or as a means of handling him?

How do you leave an elevator when you are with business associates? Do you insist on being the last one off because of the innate superiority such a gracious gesture gives you? Or do you walk off first, allowing the others to please you, taking their courtesy as if it were your due? Or do you jockey for position? "You first." "No, you."

Which of all of these is the most balanced behavior? Which does the perfectly secure man indulge in? Think about each one. Your guess is as good as a trained psychologist's. This is still a beginning science.

Where do you position yourself in a lecture hall? At the back where there is a certain amount of anonymity, even though you may miss some fine points of the lecture, or up front where you can hear and see comfortably but where you are also conspicuous?

How do you function at an informal gathering? Do you tie up your nervous hands with a drink? Do you lean against a mantel for security? It can serve as an immobilizing force for half your body and you needn't be concerned about what to say in body language—or only half concerned. Except that the very way you lean is betraying you!

Where do you sit? In a chair in the corner? In a group of your friends, or near a stranger? Which is safe and which is more interesting? Which spells security and which spells maturity?

Start observing at the next party you go to: Who are the people who dominate the gathering? Why? How much is due to body language and what gestures do they use to do it?

Notice how people sit in subway cars: How do they space themselves when the car is uncrowded? How do they cross their legs, feet and arms?

Hold the glance of a stranger a fraction longer than is necessary and see what happens. You may be in for a rude experience, and on the other hand, you may have a few good experiences. You may find yourself speaking to perfect strangers and liking it.

You know the groundwork and some of the rules. You've been playing the game of body language unconsciously all of your lifetime. Now start playing it consciously. Break a few rules and see what happens. It will be surprising and sometimes a bit frightening, adventurous, revealing and funny, but I promise you it won't be dull.

Selected References

ARDREY, R., *The Territorial Imperative*. New York: Athenium, 1966.
BIRDWHISTELL, R. L., Background to Kinesics, *ETC: A Review of General Semantics*, Vol. 13, No. 1, Autumn 1955.
—— Introduction to Kinesics. University of Louisville Press, 1952.
—— The Kinesic Level in the Investigation of the Emotions. *Expression of the Emotions in Man*. New York: International Universities Press, 1963.
BRUNER, J. S.; TAGUIRI, R., The Perception of People. *Handbook of Social Psychology*. Cambridge, Mass.: Addison Wesley, 1954.
CARPENTER, C. R., Territoriality: A Review of Concepts and Problems. *Behavior and Evolution*. New Haven: University Press, 1958.
CARPENTER, E.; McLUHAN, M., *Explorations in Communication*. Boston: Beacon Press, 1968.
CHERRY, C., *On Human Communication*. New York: Science Editions, Inc., 1961.
DARWIN, C., *The Expression of the Emotions in Man and Animals*. London, Murray, 1872.
DEUTSCH, F., Analytic Posturology, *Psychoanalytical Quarterly*, Vol. 21, 1952.
DITTMAN, A.; PARLOFF, M.; BOOMER, D., Facial and Bodily Expression: A Study of Receptivity of Emotional Cues, *Psychiatry*, Vol. 28, 1965.
EKMAN, P.; SORENSON, E. R.; FRIESEN, W. V., Pan-Cultural Elements in Facial Displays of Emotion. *Science*, Vol. 164, No. 3875, April 4, 1969.
FRANK, L. K., Tactile Communications. *ETC, A Review of General Semantics*, Vol. 16, 1958.